P9-DMH-280

COLLEGE
MONTPELIER, VT.

A SPARK LIGHTED
IN PORTLAND

A SPARK LIGHTED IN PORTLAND

THE RECORD OF THE NATIONAL BOARD OF FIRE UNDERWRITERS

A. L. TODD

McGRAW-HILL BOOK COMPANY
New York/Toronto/London

A SPARK LIGHTED IN PORTLAND

The Record of the National Board of Fire Underwriters

Library of Congress Catalog Card Number: 65-28512

FIRST EDITION

64931

CONTENTS

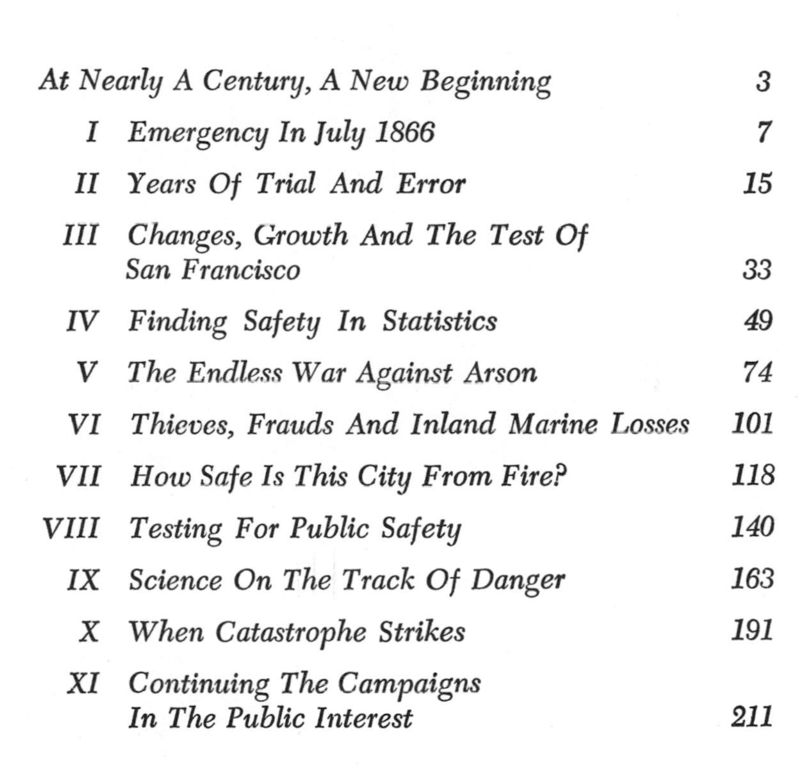

A SPARK LIGHTED IN PORTLAND

AT NEARLY A CENTURY, A NEW BEGINNING

LIKE COMMENCEMENT DAY at an institution of learning, January 1, 1965, was a symbolic date marking both a formal ending and a new beginning.

On that day, after ninety-eight and a half years of independent existence, the National Board of Fire Underwriters came officially to the end of its life. Until that moment it was America's oldest national business association. But it was far from dead. Officially coming into being from the National Board and from two other organizations with which it merged was the new American Insurance Association. So in a sense it was reborn.

The old name is now gone, but it is bound to live on in the memory of its thousands of friends, who will continue their interest in the National Board of Fire Underwriters in its new, enlarged form. For when an organization has established the kind of reputation that the National Board won for itself through long decades of enlightened services to the insurance business and to the entire American people, its part in our national life is not quickly forgotten. The old friends of the National Board recognize that it is by no means gone completely from the American scene—only that it has been transformed into something new, and that with the merger into the American Insurance Association its activities are destined to continue indefinitely into the future.

This time of transition for the National Board of Fire Underwriters is the apposite moment in which to sum up its accomplishments and to evaluate its impact on our society. Its life span of just a little short of a full century, extending from the summer of 1866 until the beginning of 1965, has been that of tremendous growth in the country's population, material wealth and economic activity. The National Board was formed at a time of relatively primitive business organization, by individual companies tentatively banding together for a limited program of mutual aid. It passes into a new and more sophisticated form in a day when American business has become accustomed to maintaining a multitude of services and cooperative activities. It was born in the era of the kerosene lantern and gaslight, when most Americans lived on the farm or in small towns. Its end and new beginning come in the day of atomic reactors, of jet flight, of electric power and petroleum fuels, when the majority of our people are thoroughly urbanized. The separate life of the National Board opened in the uncomplicated world of Currier & Ives prints; it winds up with live pictures telecast from outer space. The century since its beginning has been truly revolutionary.

Through this long and eventful period the National Board grew in strength and matured in outlook to the point where it became an almost indispensable public service institution while remaining, paradoxically, an organization of private business. Its purposes, at their origin, were frankly those of the capital stock fire insurance companies. But through the years the organization by trial and error came to realize how much the path to enlightened self-interest was also the path of the public interest. In consequence, because of the special nature of the insurance business, the purposes and programs of the National Board drew ever closer to those of the entire American people, whether insurance policyholders or not. Yet because the National Board of Fire Underwriters has always gone about its work quietly, the overwhelming majority of Americans remained largely unaware of its many services, direct and indirect, in behalf of their safety and security.

Published in celebration of its centennial year, this history of the National Board of Fire Underwriters is the story of an unusual evolution virtually unparalleled in the entrepreneurial development of the United States. It explains why the insurance business has led the country to new standards in fire prevention and fire protection for every community, to the drafting and strengthening of building codes, to the development of fire safety engineering, to the testing of new products to insure the safety of the people who use them. It shows the many hundreds of ways in which the National Board's work has made life more secure for everyone—the typical woman in her home, the worker on the job, the child in school, the patient in the hospital. It unfolds the story of an association that has taken initiative to organize and unite the forces warring on fire waste, to lessen the dangers from explosion, and to reduce property losses from such natural perils as hurricane, tornado and earthquake.

Much of this history is told in the present tense, as if the National Board of Fire Underwriters were still operating under its old name. It is told in that way in order to emphasize the fact that its work is being carried on under the banner of the American Insurance Association. Of course, certain internal changes of form and title are inevitable upon the merging of the National Board with the Association of Casualty and Surety Companies and with an organization of company executives entitled the American Insurance Association, the same name as that adopted by the newly merged group. In describing the life of the National Board of Fire Underwriters as if it were still a separate entity, the author seeks to convey its full significance at its highest point of development. To capture and to preserve its memory at such a moment fulfill the real purpose of the study of history.

Here, then, is the record of the National Board of Fire Underwriters.

I

EMERGENCY IN JULY 1866

WHEN ONE LOOKS BACK on it casually from the distance of a century, the organization of the National Board of Fire Underwriters in 1866 may seem almost like an accident. Yet when it is considered within the general context of the rapid growth of American business from the start of the Civil War onward, the birth of the National Board appears a logical, almost an inevitable, event. For a national trade association comes into being when the requirements of local business grow and evolve to the point where businessmen see a purpose in drawing together for their common benefit. In the fire insurance industry this point was reached early in 1866.

On April 30 of that year, toward the end of a meeting of the New York Board of Fire Insurance Companies held at 156 Broadway, J. Milton Smith of the Arctic Fire Insurance Company offered a motion of which the consequences were to lead far beyond his immediate purpose, and to the founding of America's first national trade association. Secretary Frank W. Ballard of the New York board recorded the event prosaically in the minute book:

> On motion of Mr. J. M. Smith a Special Committee of three, representing Companies doing an Agency business, was appointed, to confer with Companies of other cities with reference to instructions to Agents on the subject of uniform rates and commissions.
>
> The President appointed, as such Committee, Messrs. Heald, Hope & Crowell.

Behind Mr. Smith's motion lay a mounting concern felt by many insurance men over the growing seriousness of the problems which they all had to face merely to stay in business. As the New York board members saw the situation, the health of their business depended upon a fair spread between the premiums coming into their offices and the commissions paid out. This spread had to be sufficient to cover fire losses, plus operating expenses, plus profit. Fire losses and expenses were going up, and consequently profits were being squeezed. At almost every meeting of groups such as the New York Board of Fire Insurance Companies, loud calls had been sounded to the effect that "something should be done." Yet no real action was taken until Smith's resolution in April 1866.

The deadly cutthroat competition of the insurance market place, forcing premium rates down and agents' commissions up, and to which Smith's initiative was solely addressed, was but one of a triangle of forces that were choking the profit from the fire insurance industry. The second was the pressure of regulatory legislation enacted by the several states; and the third was the increasing toll of fire damage accompanying the final stage of the Civil War and the first months of peacetime.

In 1866 there were almost no established practices, either local or national, that made for stability in the fire insurance business. The companies, each acting separately, had been trying without much success to maintain a ceiling over the commissions they paid to agents and to place a floor under the rates they collected from the insured. A good agent, well placed and influential in his community, could hold up the several companies that he represented in a kind of personal auction for his services. On the other hand, competing companies in pursuit of the big policies covering choice commercial properties often found themselves forced, or sorely tempted, to undercut one another's rates, until the margin left to the successful company was dangerously low.

The second concern of the fire insurance business, restrictive legislation, arose from the indiscriminate attempts by state legislatures to protect the people of their states against fraudulent agents and incompetent companies. In the 1860s almost anyone could start an insurance company, the undercapitalized along with the well financed. Scoundrels as well as honest men could open insurance agencies and solicit business. In this sort of commercial no-man's land, the ruthless competition that logically emerged was most harmful to the established, responsible companies; their reputations suffered when either mismanagement or the heavy volume of claims from a big conflagration drove weaker companies into default and out of business. When word of such disasters spread and the public became incensed, state legislatures often responded by enacting crudely drawn laws aimed at the entire fire insurance business, hampering its growth.

As to the mounting toll of fire losses, although national statistics were far from complete, it was obvious from the claims records of many insurance companies that in the last years of the Civil War and the early months of peacetime, destruction by fire had been growing at an alarming rate. It was estimated that the national fire bill had leaped from $29,000,000 in 1864 to $43,000,000 in 1865, and there were already signs that the 1866 total would mount considerably higher. The moral breakdown that always accompanies war within a certain section of the population was clearly in evidence, particularly in the proven cases of incendiarism and fraud fires. Under the forced draft of wartime demands, industry had grown swiftly. In manufacturing cities and towns, population and wealth had rapidly increased and new construction was being rushed to completion. Because the American people were more conscious than ever before of the dollar value of their property, the demand for fire insurance was growing apace. But for some unaccountable reason fire losses seemed to be devouring the new premiums of the expanding business.

The time, therefore, was ripe for the insurance companies to consider taking some form of cooperative action in order to face a chaotic and dangerous situation that was threatening a business suddenly grown terribly hazardous to its investors. In fact, even before the Smith motion at the April 30, 1866, meeting of the New York board, a number of companies had considered trying to bring about the enactment of federal legislation that would establish the national status of fire insurance.

The three men appointed to carry out Mr. Smith's resolution were Daniel A. Heald, general agent of the Home Insurance Company, and a lawyer by training; President George T. Hope of the Continental Insurance Company; and E. W. Crowell, vice president of the Phenix Insurance Company, who was appointed chairman of the committee. Perhaps the determining reason why the action initiated by this small group led onward to greater and lasting results was the generally felt need of the times. But, in addition, Heald, Hope and Crowell from all available records seem to have been three outstanding figures within the insurance business, far above the ordinary in ability and distinction. As a consequence, when they brought in their proposal for a step forward beyond the old, familiar deploring of a sad situation, it was treated with the unusual respect that these three men commanded among their New York colleagues.

After holding several meetings during that spring of 1866, the Crowell committee circulated to the fire insurance business at large outside New York an announcement stating that in its opinion the nation's insurance companies should get together in convention in order to confer on "such measures as will be of common benefit and general interest to the underwriting interests of the country." The committee, in effect, was asking each company: Will you take part? All companies interested were to designate a representative to meet with a delegation of the New York board, at which conference plans for a national organization would be worked out.

Just as this call was being circulated, news of a tremendous conflagration in Portland, Maine, sent a shudder of fear through the fire insurance business. The fire started about 4:30 P.M. on the Fourth of July in a boat shop on Commercial Street, where a firecracker went off amid flammable materials. A strong south wind quickly fanned the fire, carrying it through the heart of the port city, where it swept away block after block of frame, brick and stone buildings in its relentless fury. By the time the fire had been stopped, the destruction marked a triangular swath nearly a half-mile long. Ten thousand Portland citizens were homeless, and the insured loss was upward of $5,000,000, roughly half the total loss.

Sympathetic citizens in many parts of the country

quickly organized public subscriptions to raise relief funds for the Portland sufferers. Simultaneously rumors began to fly to the effect that many Portland insurance claims would not be paid because companies had been driven to the wall by the disaster. To quell such assertions, representatives of several insurance companies operating in New England and New York held a meeting on July 7 in New York City, at which the group passed resolutions declaring that all Portland claims would be paid. The information was made public through the newspapers at once. Further, the insurance men insisted that premium rates should be raised, on the ground that the Portland experience demonstrated that they had been too low in the past for the security of both stockholders and policyowners.

Even more significant, the meeting resolved that participating companies should instruct local agents in Portland "to form immediately a Board of Underwriters to adopt a tariff of rates to be approved by a committee of five of the companies here represented," and that "an advance of at least 50 per cent be charged upon all risks, and that no merchandise risks be taken at less than 70 cents" (per $100 of insurance). Already acting like a national organization under the pressure of extraordinary events, the July 7 emergency meeting backed up the committee of three and impelled it to act at once to call the contemplated national conference of underwriters, to be held eleven days later in the New York board headquarters. It was obvious that the spirit of cooperation had matured, that the time had arrived to organize on a national scale.

The meeting that opened on July 18, 1866, became the historic founding convention of the National Board of Fire Underwriters. Representatives of seventy-five companies were in their chairs when Chairman Crowell called for order and turned over the gavel to the permanent chairman of the gathering, President Mark Howard of the Merchants Insurance Company of Hartford. Mr. Heald then took the floor to explain a plan of organization that would turn this *ad hoc* gathering of insurance executives into a permanent body, with a constitution and a program of year-round activities. Following his lead, the assembly on the following day voted approval of a preamble and constitution reported by a sixteen-man committee that had worked out its details overnight.

Thus, formally, was born the National Board of Fire Underwriters of the United States, to give its full title as written down on July 19, 1866. Contemporary records make it clear that Daniel A. Heald, who proposed the organizational plan and drafted the National Board constitution, was its outstanding moving spirit in the founding days. Although many others played important roles in its opening stages, his leadership fairly entitles him to be called the "father of the National Board."

The common purposes of the men who came together in 1866 are expressed in this statement of four objectives, which they approved:

1. To establish and maintain, as far as practicable, a system of uniform rates of premium;
2. To establish and maintain a uniform rate of compensation to agents and brokers;
3. To repress incendiarism and arson by combining in suitable measures for the apprehension, conviction, and punishment of criminals engaged in this nefarious business;
4. To devise and give effect to measures for the protection of our common interests and the promotion of our general prosperity.

Of these four basic objectives drawn up a century ago, the first two have long since been discarded; the third is still pursued, although in ways far more subtle than those suggested by the vigilante-style wording of the original statement of purpose; and the fourth is a generality which only barely suggests the great variety of mutual-benefit activities coming under its shadow today.

Most striking of all, however, the four-point statement of the last century is completely lacking in that broad concept of public service which lies at the heart of today's National Board program. How the organization grew, how its purposes matured through the years, and why, are the inner themes of this centennial history.

II

YEARS OF TRIAL AND ERROR

FROM THE VERY OUTSET, with its constitution and statement of purposes down on the record, the National Board of Fire Underwriters worked primarily through committees. The Executive Committee of twenty-one members named at the July convention in New York City held its first meeting in Hartford on August 9, 1866. It at once set up subcommittees as its working teams, each corresponding to problems facing the fire insurance business. The original subcommittees were those on Finance; on Local Boards, Rates, and Commissions; on Cooperation of Companies; on Incendiarism and Arson; and on Legislation and Taxation.

As early as the first Executive Committee meeting it was evident that the brave words of the founding convention might be more difficult to apply than some of the founders at first recognized. The New York meeting had resolved that agents should be paid a maximum commission of 10 per cent on all risks except dwellings and "outbuildings," meaning sheds and barns, for which 15 per cent should be the maximum. But the record of the August meeting in Hartford shows Mr. Crowell offering a resolution stating that:

> . . . in the opinion of the committee, it is deemed expedient to postpone the application of the resolution respecting agents' commission.

The resolution was adopted. Clearly, the army of agents on which the insurance business depended had let their complaints be heard at the top level of the member companies. The latter were not yet confident of their power to enforce the ceiling on commissions which they earnestly desired.

Despite this initial setback on the matter of commissions, organization of the National Board proceeded rapidly. At the annual meeting held in February 1867 the Executive Committee reported that ninety-nine companies and thirty-two local boards were represented. Most interesting news of all was that local agents in many cities and districts understood the wisdom of cooperating so as to bring order, at least on a local scale, to a chaotic business. The Executive Committee noted that within the few months since the National Board had been formed "over two hundred local boards, with rates more or less advanced, and uniform in character, have been organized under the auspices of the Executive Committee of this board, and the favorable results are apparent to all."

It is clear that in its early years the National Board was essentially an organization for rate control. Indeed, its most important activity lay in promoting the establishment of boards of local agents and enlisting them in the cause of setting up and maintaining uniform rates for risks underwritten in their sales area. It seemed of little consequence, for example, that rates should differ between two mills of similar construction turning out the same manufactured goods if one of them, say, were in Manchester, New Hampshire, and the other in Rochester, New York. What mattered most to the industry as a whole, as reflected in National Board discussions, was that all agents in Manchester should stick to their agreed-upon premium rates and that the Rochester agents should do the same in their own city.

Within the first two years 475 local boards had been organized, all pledged to the National Board policies of uniformity within their jurisdiction. Simultaneously, the National Board set about formulating standards by which the most important classifications of risk could be rated. In order to do this it began to make statistical studies through special committees to determine just what was the degree of fire risk inherent in the use of kerosene, of illuminating gas, and other technical innovations. At the start these studies were quite primitive, but they represented an attempt to study fire risks on a more sound mathematical basis than ever before.

The benefits of association had now become so obvious within the insurance business that by the 1869 meeting tables of rates had been prepared for 1824 places in the United States. At this point the National Board set up a rating bureau, which divided the country into six departments, each with its department committee, office and staff. With the spread of standardization, rates generally had been raised to the point where the industry was enjoying prosperity. To protect it, thirty-seven companies even joined in signing what came to be known as the "Chicago Compact," a solemn pledge to remove any local agent upon a second conviction for violating the scale of rates approved by the National Board.

Already the new state of things had become too good to last. Agents here and there began rate cutting in the same old way, and the companies to which they brought business balked at discharging them. Various proposals were sounded within the National Board for coercing companies to enforce the rules, but they echoed hollowly in the air of a free enterprise economy. The American businessman was simply too much of an individualist to listen seriously to them. By December of 1869 Chairman E. W. Crowell of the Executive Committee was forced to acknowledge that:

> The outside public being made aware that our hold on local boards is not as strong as formerly, have redoubled their efforts for cheaper insurance, and many companies are giving discretionary power to their agents to meet this demand. If this demoralization goes much further . . . it is only a question of time when, in all of the principal places at least, the matter of rates will be a thing of the past.

The full circle was closed at the meeting of the Executive Committee on February 24, 1870, a scant three and one-half years after the foundation of the National Board. At this session the committee authorized local boards to "modify, suspend, or declare advisory any or all rates fixed by them." Thus, what had been obligatory became purely optional. As an effective rate-fixing agency, the National Board had tried, but it had failed.

Meanwhile, during this same period, the National Board was much concerned over harassment of the insurance business by a multiplicity of state laws. Strange as it may seem today, the National Board sought relief by attempting to bring fire insurance under federal law, using a test case in the state of Virginia as the vehicle. In May of 1866, just as the New York founders of the National Board were laying the groundwork for the first meeting, an insurance agent named Samuel B. Paul in Petersburg, Virginia, was seeking a court test of a new state law. This statute required the licensing and bonding of agents within the state who represented "foreign," or non-Virginia, insurance companies. Paul represented Germania, Hanover, Niagara and Republic Insurance Companies of New York. Acting on the principle that the extremely high personal bond required by the Virginia statute was an impediment to interstate commerce, Paul refused to deposit the bond, although he complied with the other requirements of registration. When Paul issued a $3000 policy without having put up his bond, he was convicted in a Petersburg court for this specific offense.

In order to test whether a state law regulating insurance by "foreign" companies was constitutional, the National Board of Fire Underwriters assisted Paul in appealing from his Virginia conviction to the Supreme Court of the United States. The annual meeting of the National Board in April 1869 agreed to an assessment for expenses in the Paul case up to $15,000. Many insurance men hoped that the high court would lead them out of their legislative troubles by ruling that issuance of a fire insurance policy to a citizen of one state by a company based in another state constituted interstate commerce. Such a ruling by the Supreme Court, the insurance men believed, would clear the way for enactment by Congress of sound federal insurance law that would encourage the growth of the business. The somewhat naive confidence of the members of the National Board Committee on Legislation and Taxation that their view would prevail in the Supreme Court is illustrated by this passage from its report to the April 1869 meeting:

> Your Committee feel authorized . . . to express strong hopes of obtaining a decision in favor on the ground held by members of the National Board, namely, that underwriting is inseparable from, and constitutes a part of, the commerce of the country . . .

This position is set forth by your Committee on all occasions as one about which there is no diversity of opinion among the members of the Board; and your Committee urge that the unanimous opinion of so large a body of intelligent men, familiar with the subject, in favor of the position named, should give it weight worthy to influence the judgment of the Supreme Court as to the interpretation of Commercial Law.

The high court in Washington heard argument on the case, now known in legal history as *Paul v. Virginia,* on October 12, 1869. The gist of the state's position is made clear in this sentence from the brief submitted by Virginia to the Supreme Court:

No foreign insurance company has a right to come into Virginia by her agents, to do the business of insurance, without the consent of Virginia, and, in giving her consent, she has the perfect right to impose such reasonable conditions as she may deem necessary and proper to secure the payment of her revenue and the security of her citizens from imposition and frauds.

On November 1, 1869, Justice Stephen J. Field, speaking for a unanimous Supreme Court, dashed the industry's hopes. Regulation of the fire insurance business, the court ruled, was purely a state matter, not within federal jurisdiction. The salient passage in Justice Field's opinion, which was to stand for many years as a keystone decision in American insurance law, declared:

Issuing a policy of insurance is not a transaction of commerce. The policies are simply contracts of indemnity against loss by fire, entered into between the corporations and the assured, for a consideration paid by the latter. These contracts are not articles of commerce in any proper meaning of the word... They are, then, local transactions, and are governed by the local law. They do not constitute a part of the commerce between the States any more than a contract for the purchase and sale of goods in Virginia by a citizen of New York whilst in Virginia would constitute a portion of such commerce.

Having hoped for, even expected, so much from the Supreme Court, the National Board was deeply disappointed by its defeat. Shortly after the event the Committee on Legislation and Taxation commented ruefully that its members:

> ... would not presume to criticize the opinion of so learned a body as is the Supreme Court of the U.S. They, however, feel it to be entirely consistent with a submissive spirit to murmur their disappointment at the result stated.
>
> And when they remember that Underwriting owes its inception to the necessities of commerce, and is today one of its principal safeguards and promoters, they feel constrained to admit that the language of the decision in which it is declared that Underwriting is in no sense an element of commerce, is in conflict with the irresistible convictions of common sense.
>
> Your Committee would not, however, bespatter the judicial ermine with suggestions drawn from so humble and unpopular a basis of judgment as common sense confessedly is.

As one looks back on these words of sarcasm from the vantage point of the mid-twentieth century, it is indeed ironic to view the deep regret of insurance men over the court's having denied their business the remedy they sought—federal regulation—by its ruling in *Paul v. Virginia!* Soon enough, however, they were to bless the memory of Justice Field and his Supreme Court colleagues for what they did that day.

With the loss of this test case simultaneous with the collapse of its attempts to regulate premium rates by policing insurance agents, the National Board in 1870 sank into a dark period. Company interest flagged, dues payments fell off, and for lack of funds the National Board secretary was dismissed. The small office in New York was practically deserted. William H. Post, the headquarters clerk, recalled later that for most of two years "I was alone in the little office at 156 Broadway; all I had to do was to draw my salary, pay the janitor every month, and the rent every three months."

But the calm was suddenly shattered by one supremely dramatic and tragic event that awoke the entire country to a realization of the tremendous ruin that fire could visit without warning on a great city. That event was the great Chicago fire of October 8 to 10, 1871, which by song and story has been woven permanently into the tapestry of American history and folklore.

It is difficult today to conceive the full emotional impact of the Chicago fire on the American people unless one views it in its context. Five years before, the great fire in Portland, Maine, had been widely advertised as the greatest, most destructive conflagration in American history. It is doubtful that this was precisely true, whether the measurement was made in terms of dollar value of destruction, number of lives lost, or the total area devastated. But the Portland fire was, by common consent, the most serious fire tragedy that had been visited on the country within most people's memory. The Chicago fire, however, was so much greater that overnight the Portland conflagration was almost forgotten. A few comparative figures reveal that the Chicago holocaust was roughly equivalent in magnitude to ten Portland fires: an estimated 15,000 buildings destroyed in Chicago, compared with 1500 in Portland; roughly three and a half square miles of the Midwestern city burned, compared with Portland's one-third of a square mile; and a Chicago dollar loss estimated at $175,000,000, compared with an estimated $10,000,000 to $12,000,000 loss in Portland.

Little wonder that the Chicago fire set men to thinking

of the common danger to life and property when once a fire in a densely packed city should get out of hand. And the public learned a hard lesson when reports spread out from Chicago that a number of the weaker companies that had issued policies in the city at rates dangerously low (to them), and in high volume, had gone bankrupt. Even the most soundly financed firms were hard put to it to make good their obligations. But the Chicago fire also had the effect of driving the surviving companies together, revivifying the National Board and many local boards. Rates were quickly advanced to the high levels of 1868, and the insuring public for a little while showed that it preferred to buy a safe policy at a somewhat higher premium than to save a few dollars on cheap insurance.

The reform lasted only a few months. The same old competitive forces were once more at work, and agents again began cutting rates, despite the official instructions of the companies and the pledged word of company spokesmen that they were observing the rules agreed upon. One National Board member in 1872 frankly challenged his colleagues with the truth about their two-faced policy:

> We have solemnly resolved at our meetings, and we have gone out and given contrary instructions to our agents . . . That is the cause of so many tariffs and rates being disregarded by agents. They have received secret instructions from their companies to disregard tariff rates.

Still shaking from the Chicago experience, the National Board in 1872 revised its constitution and bylaws, cut the Executive Committee membership down for greater efficiency and appointed Thomas H. Montgomery as general agent for the National Board. His salary, an unprecedented $10,000 a year, indicated how seriously the organization took its role as leader of the industry. Mr.

Montgomery had only begun the task of reorganizing and strengthening local boards when, on November 9, 1872, another great fire burned into the consciousness of the nation once more the lessons apparently learned in Chicago, then partly forgotten. This was the costly fire that ravaged sixty-five acres in downtown Boston, ruining 750 buildings and causing an insured loss of some $60,000,000 and an estimated loss of property worth $75,000,000.

Some companies had survived the Chicago disaster and had capitalized heavily on its emotional backlash by writing large amounts of insurance. They suffered, of course, most heavily. Again the air was filled with rumors of company failures, from which many National Board members realized that everyone in the business would suffer. But again the fire insurance business rallied around the National Board as the one instrumentality through which it could bring order and security from discord and grave danger. In the wake of the Boston fire, rates advanced 30 per cent in towns of less than fifty thousand population, and 50 per cent in larger cities. The National Board membership soon represented 90 per cent of fire insurance premiums paid in the United States. High rates and good business brought dividends on fire insurance capital of 12.73 per cent in 1874.

The two terrible disasters in Chicago and Boston taught another lesson that was destined to have an even greater long-range effect on the country. It was that the organized insurance industry had a positive duty to help prevent fires. Up to this time the prevailing attitude among insurance men held that their business consisted of calculating what the fire risks were, then selling policies at rates that would both compensate the insured and produce a profit for the underwriter. Unless he were speaking specifically about the suppression of arson, the insurance man who spoke in terms of fire prevention was a visionary ahead of his time. But the recent big city fires that had spread over large areas upset the best calculations of risk. They had already cut deeply into the resources of even the most efficiently run companies that were heavily involved in the Portland, Chicago and Boston conflagrations. And even if these companies were cautious enough not to plunge too deeply with what they considered "bad" risks, there was no telling when a fire starting ten blocks away might within a few hours sweep away a dozen of their "good" risks.

In his annual address in 1873, President Henry A. Oakley of the National Board sounded a call for the organization to turn its mind to fire prevention. He declared that with the exception of New York, no large city had a law on the books that even remotely provided for the erection of buildings that would resist fire, and even in New York the building law was administered feebly. Boston, Oakley said, had changed its building law somewhat since the fire, but it was still:

> ... far from what it should be ... It is evident, therefore, that if Boston is to be rebuilt properly, it must be outside of its laws.
>
> In Philadelphia, recent examinations have shown that glaring and outrageous evasions of even the moderately strict law of that city had been allowed by the building inspectors, whose duty it was to enforce it. Now if this be the case in our great cities, what must it be in our smaller ones?
>
> Owners of property, builders, and architects alike seem to have been wilfully blind to the immense risks they were imposing upon property ... Even the insurance interests, though somewhat alive to the danger, were afraid to assert their knowledge, and decline to insure such buildings, preferring to go

with the multitude; the penalty has been paid for this neglect of duty, at a fearful price to us all.

Oakley then proposed that the National Board of Fire Underwriters take on the job of pressing for laws that would help prevent fire. He told the meeting:

> We can do much to shape legislation that will benefit not only our own interests but the whole country, by securing such wise and salutary laws as might prevent the recurrence of other destructive conflagrations.

In recognizing that "our own interests" and those of the whole country ran together, Oakley, perhaps without fully realizing it, focused on the secret of the National Board's later success. This one sentence in his 1873 address foreshadowed the change by which the National Board was eventually to be transformed from a narrowly oriented protective business association, which it was at its birth, into the public-service institution of broad outlook that it is today. But the change was not to occur all at once.

The mid-1870s were years of innovation, as the National Board began to feel its weight, and to use it. One of the targets in the opening stages of the fire prevention war was the wooden mansard roof, which had two sloping sections on each of its four sides. For all its popularity as a sign of opulence in building, the mansard design was a fire menace. The mansard rose well above the top of the masonry walls. When fire would break out in a nearby building the mansard roof, once exposed to the fire, acted as a transmission belt for the spread of the flames to other buildings.

Another National Board target was the open elevator shaft. At this time the elevator was an innovation most commonly installed in hotels and factories. An elevator system was usually built without solid doors to seal it off from the hallways and rooms which it served. In fires, therefore, the shaft proved an effective route by which flames were drawn upward from one floor to those above.

While engaging in legislative efforts to curb bad building practice, insurance men in this period began to use another tactic as well: offering the policyholder the carrot of lower rates in order to make safe construction and good equipment pay for themselves. An entire community soon profited from this policy when the National Board instructed the local board in Rochester, New York, to cut back the 20 per cent rate advance of December 1872, because the city had opened a completely new municipal water works. The lesson that virtue paid a cash reward was not lost on the insured in other cities. Thus the property owner was given an incentive to render his property fire resistant.

In 1866, when the National Board was formed, only fifteen cities in the United States had steam fire engines; the rest were hand pumpers of very limited range. In 1876, but ten years later, two hundred and seventy-five cities were equipped with steam-powered fire engines. By this time, too, New York City had organized its first company of paid fire fighters. Other cities were either changing or considering a change from their traditional volunteer force, that was at base part social and part political, to a professional fire department, trained in its duties and responsible to the city government. The romance of the old fire laddies, with their singing and beer bouts, racing and fist fights, had to yield to the realities of modern life. Fighting fire had become too serious a business to be run by amateurs any longer.

The importance of the National Board of Fire Underwriters' role in pressing for these changes can best be illustrated by what happened in Chicago in the summer of

1874, less than three years after the great disaster in the "Windy City." Early that year the National Board had received so many disturbing reports of the bad fire conditions in rebuilt, forgetful Chicago that in June the Executive Committee appointed a special committee of two men to investigate. The committee found, first, that the city commissioners were paying most of their attention to the police department, with only minimal concern for the fire department. Discipline, training and equipment in the Chicago firehouses were appallingly bad, as though the city had never even been through the searing experience of 1871. It was found that many old and new buildings rested on timbers which were so elevated from the ground level that continuous air space partially filled with burnable debris extended throughout the block. Lumberyards and planing mills were scattered in areas where railroad locomotives were constantly throwing sparks from their stacks. Wooden buildings, the quickest and cheapest to build, had been slapped up on the ashes of the destroyed structures, and wooden sidewalks were back in place along the streets.

Upon receiving the report from its committee, the National Board at once wired its local board in Chicago urging that it pressure the city government into immediately establishing a special fire patrol of at least one hundred men, pending changes and improvements in the fire department, that it increase city water facilities, that it pass and enforce a stringent new building law, and other points. The National Board declared that if the Chicago authorities did not act on its safety demands by September 30, member companies would withdraw all insurance from the city.

At first the city government stammered and stalled, but an aroused Chicago Citizens' Committee late in September forced it to appoint a new fire department head. The fact that the National Board member companies actually carried out the threat, and canceled all fire policies in Chicago, finally spurred the city officials to efforts to improve the situation. By November 20, 1874, a National Board committee accepted an invitation to visit Chicago to see what had been accomplished. The city officials, until a few weeks before careless of fire prevention and scornful of the fire insurance industry, now rolled out the red carpet for the inspecting team. The change was so much for the better in regard to fire safety that the underwriters' ban was subsequently withdrawn. By its stand in this instance, the fire insurance industry recognized that it had tremendous influence, when mobilized, to perform a public service of the highest order.

Yet again the pendulum swung. Business had become too good; rates were too high to last for long. There was so much of a profit margin between income and outgo that agents and companies began to chip away once more at the rate structure that had firmed up since the Chicago fire. By the 1876 annual meeting the entire fire insurance industry was engaged in civil war—National Board companies pitted against non-board companies, and many of the former violating the rules while trying to disguise their apostasy. Some companies resigned in protest. More persistent loyal board men, still devoted to the rate-fixing principle, cried out that everyone should hold the line or they would all be finished. Only this time there came no act-of-God conflagration to drive them into working together. Debate over enforced premium rating waxed hot at National Board meetings, until, in April 1877, a Committee on Retrenchment recommended that yearly expenses be cut from $113,000 to $15,000. This would mean abandonment of the rating program, the principal activity of the National Board. To those veterans who had been with the organization through its eleven years of life, this abandonment seemed like a personal tragedy.

President Rudolph Garrigue of the Germania Insurance Company, speaking in favor of the cutback of National Board functions, delivered a blunt speech in which he reviewed the reasons for the organization's failure as a rate-fixing mechanism. He proposed instead that it limit itself to other goals.

"Is it not wise," he asked the group, "to preserve the vitality of the board for attainable purposes, by removing the bone of contention presented by a rigid tariff?" Garrigue said there were six other worthwhile forms of service that the National Board could perform under the reduced budget, namely: maintaining archives, collating statistics, dealing with legislation, combating arson, disseminating knowledge of fire causes and advising local boards. Later in the meeting Daniel A. Heald thoughtfully and soberly reviewed the experience of the past eleven years and declared that under the circumstances he, too, "could not vote for obligatory rates one day longer."

With the vote for retrenchment, the National Board thus gave up its attempts to control fire insurance tariffs. For the next eleven years it sank into a kind of semi-life, which some of the press interpreted, prematurely, as the calm that comes over the dying. Yet the National Board of Fire Underwriters lived on, a pale shadow of its former self. Dues were lowered to a nominal sum, just enough to cover the greatly reduced program of activity centering upon routine committee meetings, at which the faithful adherents invoked the glories and hopes of the recent past. General Agent Montgomery resigned, and the staff work at headquarters was carried on by the secretary of the Executive Committee, Henry K. Miller, who was to serve the board loyally until his death in 1910.

Some of those insurance men who had met defeat in their attempts to make the National Board a mechanism for enforcing a national standard of rates and commissions stayed with it in the expectation that its day would come around again. They tried spasmodically through the moribund years of the late seventies and eighties to set up various new rate-fixing and commission-control systems to insure their companies' prosperity, but each fell apart as its predecessor had done. Essentially, the National Board in these dim years represented just a hope for better things—for a day when the companies could again work together for their common good. But in practice the National Board was not much more than a discussion group with a letterhead.

By 1887 the spirit was so low that the organization omitted its annual meeting, for the only time in its history. Although many hoped vainly through all these years that some magical turn of events would transform the entire competitive fire insurance industry into a familial band of cooperators, by 1888 it had become quite clear to almost everyone that this would never be. The American way of doing business, at least in fire insurance, was just too independent, too individualistic, to be organized into a trust.

It was no accident that at this same time the growth of heavy industry and of business institutions throughout the country had given rise, as a countermeasure, to the anti-trust movement in American politics. No target for the anti-trust forces in the state legislature could be more obvious than a compact among insurance companies doing business within a state, under which they agreed to limit competition as far as premium rates were concerned. This was no hidden agreement, but an open compact. A so-called "anti-compact law," aimed directly at the insurance business, was introduced in the Michigan legislature in 1883. The first bill failed of passage, but Ohio passed such a law in 1885; Michigan, Nebraska and Texas soon followed, and a national tide of anti-compact laws swept upward into a flood that drowned out the last lingering hope that the National Board could effectively restrict competition. The time had come for it to turn its attention to other goals.

The 1888 and 1889 meetings, therefore, were held at the critical turn in the affairs of the organization. A line was drawn under the unsuccessful business of the past, and public service was put at the head of the National Board agenda. Nearly fifty representatives attended the 1889 meeting, in contrast to only eight delegates and twenty-five company members the previous year. A fresh spirit of optimism filled the group as it prepared to rebuild the National Board of Fire Underwriters on a thoroughly revised foundation.

III

CHANGES, GROWTH AND THE TEST OF SAN FRANCISCO

IF BY 1889 the National Board of Fire Underwriters had not already been infused with a new spirit of concentrating on reducing fire losses rather than on enforcing higher rates, the terrible destruction of that one year might alone have forced such a change. For 1889 was a year of evil destiny, as far as disastrous fires were concerned. On April 19 the city of New York suffered a conflagration that caused close to $2,000,000 damage. Then, on June 6, the Seattle, Washington, business district was burned to the extent of $7,000,000. Less than two months later thirty-five blocks in Spokane were destroyed in a $6,000,000 fire. On November 26 some sixty acres of Lynn, Massachusetts, were ravaged, with a loss of about $5,000,000. Only two days afterward a conflagration in Boston caused $2,800,000 worth of damage. In the entire country, the year's aggregate property loss by fire set a new record, exceeding $123,000,000. In the face of such a toll, the insurance industry felt that it must take action against the rising tide of fire loss, and it wasted no time in going to work.

The National Board promptly authorized its Committee on Fire Departments, Fire Patrol and Water Supply to hire an expert "to examine into the present condition and needs of the fire departments and fire facilities throughout the country." Assistant Chief John W. Smith of the fire department of Brooklyn, New York, was consequently engaged as inspector of fire departments for the National Board. So it came about that fully fifteen years after the National Board had forced the city of Chicago to meet its standards for fire protection in the showdown of 1874, the organization set up permanent machinery by which it could observe city fire departments continuously, and on a national scale.

The year 1892 found the National Board greatly rejuvenated, with an enlarged membership and a fresh, optimistic approach toward its mission and its future. Daniel A. Heald, the primary figure in the founding of the National Board in 1866 and the man who had held the presidency from 1881 through most of its dark winter years, happily had stayed in office until 1891, long enough to witness its renaissance. He was succeeded by DeWitt Clinton Skilton of the Phoenix (of Hartford), who emphasized in his presidential address to the 1892 meeting of the National Board how much the old outlook toward fire insurance had given way, under pressure of increasing fire loss and mounting resistance to higher premiums, to emphasis on fire prevention. President Skilton put the modern concept of fire insurance to the meeting this way:

> The old theory . . . that a risk should be written as found, and a rate adequate to the hazard be charged, is fast becoming obsolete, and today all local and district associations, and all syndicates for writing great industries are aiming to secure

improvements in construction and greater care, and all favor the introduction of automatic and other appliances for the prevention and extinguishing of fires, the inducement to the assured being a greatly reduced rate for the lessening of this hazard.

This passage in Skilton's address of 1892 stands in sharp contrast to the prevailing atmosphere of the original National Board meeting in 1866. Twenty-six years before theirs had been a spirit of grouping together for mutual defense of their investments; now they were looking outward for ways of rendering greater public service. Then they had united in order to raise rates; now they were trying to make it possible to reduce rates.

Other signs of the new spirit were manifest in the National Board's approaches to President Benjamin Harrison, and to Congress, to the end that fire prevention might be made a matter of national concern by means of a federal government investigation of fire causes, building construction and the regulation of special hazards. In addition, letters were sent to governors and to state insurance commissioners, asking their cooperation in the same effort. The National Board also published and distributed a pamphlet on fire waste, an act that was the beginning of its public education program, which was to flower through the years and eventually reach into virtually every schoolroom, place of employment and home.

The National Board at this time also held a technical conference with a committee of architects, builders and fire engineers on practical steps to improve construction from a fire-safety viewpoint. From the meeting came a draft model building law for the State of New York. The bill encompassing it was at first defeated in the state legislature, but copies of the proposed New York law were circulated widely. The first draft was superseded by an 1896 revision known as the "National Board's Model Building

Law," which at last gave the lay public as well as specialists in all states a precise objective on which to focus the drive to prevent and to control building fires.

Together, these actions by the National Board betokened a willingness to accept national leadership in the endless war against fire waste, by assuming the moral responsibility for taking initiative, and encouraging others to join in, each in the way best suited to his abilities. The National Board was simply proving again the old rule that leadership in human affairs goes to the one who takes the initiative.

It was in the late eighties and early nineties that America became aware of the new fire danger represented by electricity. When electricity first came into use, it was commonly believed that its employment in buildings as a source of light would greatly reduce fire peril, because it would replace kerosene oil and gas, the known cause of thousands upon thousands of fires. Yet strangely enough the fire insurance industry discovered that some of the finest buildings, owned by people considered the very best risks, were burning—without apparent cause. It was observed that these buildings had been wired for electricity. The suspicion then spread that electricity might be causing fires in some mysterious fashion which those without technical training could not completely understand. An example of the way this new and perplexing problem struck one National Board member can be illustrated by the following quotation, taken from the minutes of one of the meetings, which today seems somewhat quaint but in 1890 reflected the concern and perplexity gripping the industry:

> We cannot assume that the most reputable merchants have all at once become criminals. We find that our better class of risks is burning in a greater ratio than ever before, and that

there are mysterious causes at work, which we do not understand . . . That mysterious element I believe to be electricity . . . I believe this is what is burning us out, and running up our mortality rate to such an unprecedented figure . . . We are standing, I repeat, in the presence of a mysterious element which no one is at present able to fathom.

It was not long before engineers generally recognized the totally new fire dangers inherent in the overloaded wire, insufficient insulation and the electrical short circuit. On August 17, 1892, the National Board called an emergency meeting of electrical inspectors for the insurance industry to determine how the companies should meet the menace of this new technology which was being put into general use before the average person knew how to employ it with safety. From this meeting was formed a group called the Underwriters International Electrical Association, which formulated a National Board Electric Code to govern safe installations.

From that time on the National Board engaged staff engineers to study electricity in relation to fire safety. Their studies resulted in a flow of illustrated reports from the National Board headquarters which not only were read by the underwriters but were passed from them to builders, building owners, contractors and mechanics. Virtually all the laws and codes covering safe electrical installation in the years that have followed can be traced back to this pioneering by the National Board. One can only speculate how serious the situation might have become in the early years of the electrical era if the National Board had not been on the scene, and organized so as to offer leadership in the cooperative effort to prevent fires of electrical origin.

One of the engineers who came to the National Board in this early period of the electrical era was Wilbur E.

Mallalieu. With a degree in mechanical engineering from Stevens Institute, Mallalieu, then twenty-six years of age, was hired in 1900 as an electrical inspector and engineer until 1910, when he was promoted to head the National Board staff. His title at the time, General Agent, was soon changed to General Manager. Mallalieu was to hold that position for forty years, until his retirement in 1950. In his long service through the organization's most dynamic period of growth, during which the staff increased from 6 to 350, Wilbur E. Mallalieu in a sense came to personify the National Board of Fire Underwriters.

In this period the National Board and its member companies severally were enjoying considerable success in enlisting allies both within and without the insurance field for the war against fire. In 1896 a group of technical men in the stock companies formed the National Fire Protection Association, devoted exclusively to engineering work aimed at fire prevention. At first the activities of the NFPA centered on the study of performance standards for such equipment as automatic sprinklers, fire extinguishers and fireproof doors (as fire doors were then called). Immediately appreciating the value of this work, the National Board lent a helping hand by appropriating $1000 to print and distribute the findings of the new organization's experiments.

Simultaneously, the National Board acted as the forum in which technical men and business leaders could discuss the emergent body of theory and practice making up the science of fire prevention, which was now struggling toward maturity. In its meetings effective decisions could be reached on ways in which to apply the newly acquired knowledge. After a series of conferences, the National Board late in 1899 decided to set up its own Board of Consulting Engineers whose duty it would be to recommend fire prevention standards and rules to the Executive Committee. Once adopted, these decisions would be advocated by members of the National Board in their dealings with policyholders.

Making great strides forward by pursuing public service activities, the National Board grew steadily during the next few busy years. The 1901 meeting found 129 companies on the rolls, compared with only 104 in 1896, and in sharp contrast to the lonely twenty-five of 1888. Its prestige and influence were at a high mark; 125 municipal governments had adopted and were enforcing the National Electrical Code, which the National Board had revised in the late nineties as a result of accumulated experience with electricity.

It was in this same year, 1901, that the organization finally cut from its statement of purposes the outmoded parts relating to promoting uniform premium rates through activating local boards. The National Board's reason for being, as successive changes had remade it from the original four points, now read this way:

1. To promote harmony, correct practices, and the principles of sound underwriting. To devise and give effect to measures for the protection of the common interests, and the promotion of such laws and regulations as will secure stability and solidity to capital employed in the business of fire insurance, and protect it against oppressive, unjust, and discriminative legislation.

2. To repress incendiarism and arson by combining in suitable measures for the apprehension, conviction and punishment of criminals guilty of that crime.

3. To gather such statistics and establish such classification of hazards as may be for the interest of members.

4. To secure the adoption of uniform and correct policy forms and clauses and to endeavor to agree upon such rules and regulations in reference to the adjustment of losses as may be desirable and in the interest of all concerned.

5. To influence the introduction of improved and safe methods of building construction, encourage the adoption of fire-protective measures, secure efficient organization and equipment of Fire Departments, with adequate and improved water systems, and establish rules designed to regulate all hazards constituting a menace to the business. Every member shall be bound in honor to cooperate with every other member to accomplish the desired objects and purposes of the board.

The first and second points in the original statement of purpose, relating to the pursuit of uniform rates and commissions, were now completely gone. The third point, on repression of incendiarism and arson, remained as in 1866 except for a minor change in wording. The significant evolution through thirty-five years of the National Board's life could be seen in the expansion of the old fourth point, on promoting the common good of National Board members. Now the statement of purpose listed a variety of activities not mentioned at all in the 1866 declaration. These included: promoting constructive legislation; gathering statistics on which to base sound underwriting by classification of hazards; reaching agreement on the content of policies and on adjustment of losses; and, finally, the all-important matter of taking the lead in the repression of fires by a variety of means.

With the turn of the century, the National Board of Fire Underwriters appears from this statement to have completed the process of breaking away from its infant and childhood stages and was assuming its responsibilities as an adult organization. Put another way—it can be said to have turned its back on the self-service concept of the old era before most other business organizations did, and to have embraced the public service concept that is characteristic of American industry in the twentieth century. Fortunately so, because the next big test for the National Board and the entire industry was not long in coming.

Almost every year since the rash of great urban conflagrations in 1889 there had been big fires causing upward of a million dollars' worth of damage. But in 1904 and 1906 there occurred a double blow reminiscent of the Chicago and Boston disasters in the early seventies. This was the close sequence of the great fire in Baltimore, then the earthquake followed by fire in San Francisco—still the greatest city fire on record in America.

The Baltimore conflagration struck the most valuable part of the business district, burning through February 7 and 8, 1904, and either sweeping away or gutting all construction over an area of eighty city blocks. With damage estimated in the neighborhood of fifty million dollars, the Baltimore fire was the biggest conflagration in the thirty-three years since the Chicago holocaust. Also in 1904 other big fires caused tremendous losses in Toronto, in Rochester, New York, in Yazoo City, Mississippi, and in Sioux City, Iowa. And within the same period of a few months the entire nation was shocked by two other fire tragedies that took a tremendous toll of human life. They were the Iroquois Theatre fire in Chicago on the afternoon of December 30, 1903, costing more than 600 lives; and the burning and sinking of the holiday cruiser the S. S. *General Slocum* in New York Harbor, taking more than one thousand victims.

By their sheer volume and recurring frequency, almost as if they came inevitably like the seasons, these fire disasters impressed themselves deeply into the public consciousness. Magazine and newspaper editors were shocked for the first time into realizing that fire prevention and fire safety had become subjects of general, rather than special, concern. Their pages began to feature articles on fire safety in places of public assembly, as well as in the factory, office and home. The following are titles typical of many that appeared in general circulation magazines from the time of the Iroquois Theatre fire, deploring America's miserably bad fire record:

"Burnt Money," "Combustible America," "Fire—an American Extravagance," "Land of Fire," "Our Enormous Fire Losses," "Red Plague," and "Waste by Fire."

This new wave of public education and criticism did not stop at deploring a bad situation; it stressed what people could do to protect lives and property by teaching them where the dangers of fire lay and what corrective action should be taken. Typical titles of articles of this kind included:

"Chicago Theatre Fire Drill," "Factory Fire Drills," "Hotels and Fire Drills," "Building Against Fire," "Dangers Lurking in Woodpiles," "Fire Resisting Building Materials," "Facts on Fire Prevention," "Spontaneous Combustion as a Fire Hazard," and even "How Not to Have Fires."

In the twenty-seven months following the Iroquois Theatre fire, the message was thus brought to the man in the street that fire dangers lurked everywhere—in the city and on the farm, in the quiet of one's home as well as on boat or train, in the place of amusement, the store, office, or factory. Now, at least, the average man was taught the rudimentary concepts of fire safety, and became familiar with some of the terms and concepts, such as "spontaneous combustion." He learned what a chemical fire extinguisher was for, and how to use it. As a nation we became conscious of the need for fire drills. We learned how to manipulate fire doors, and understood why school and theater doors should be built so as to open outward to a push. Americans began consciously to look for the EXIT sign when taking their seats at the theater, and they became fire-escape conscious when engaging a hotel room. The change did not take place all at once, of course, but in these years the increase in attention paid to fire prevention and fire safety represented a great step forward in public education. Actively promoting this informational campaign, as could be expected, was the National Board of Fire Underwriters.

A most important result that sprang from the ashes of Baltimore early in 1904 was the municipal inspection system of the National Board. Insurance men knew that it was impossible to prevent every fire, but they firmly believed that it was possible to contain fires more effectively and prevent their sweeping through large sections of a city. So the National Board retained an inspecting staff of trained engineers, under the leadership of E. G. Hopson, formerly of the Metropolitan Water Board of Boston. This staff set out to survey the congested centers of population in all parts of the country, and from their findings to advise both underwriters and city authorities on the ability of each municipality to control its fire hazards so as to prevent multiblock conflagrations. The program was entirely voluntary, but city fathers were eager to welcome the National Board inspectors. The engineers moved quickly into action, proceeding in teams from city to city.

On arrival in a municipality, a building expert from the team would survey the major downtown structures and note the method of construction, materials, design and spacing. He drew up a report of the conflagration danger inherent in the situation as he found it. Meanwhile, another member of the team trained in fire fighting checked the readiness of the city fire department, its manning, equipment, morale and leadership. At times he would even put some of the fire horses through speed trials to see if they were up to the firehouse job, or should, instead, be drawing milk wagons. Simultaneously, a water supply expert went carefully over the city water system, checking the supply of water, the piping, hydrants and valves. From this inspection he could determine the volume in which water could be delivered to the built-up areas in time of greatest need. Taken all together, the National Board inspection program, administered by an impartial outside agency, was exactly what many city administrations required to show them how to improve their fire-fighting systems, for no one other than the National Board had the expertise to do the job.

When the National Board team had finished its inspection and submitted its written report, city authorities who bore the Baltimore tragedy vividly in mind usually tried to make the recommended improvements. But by the time they resolved to take the first steps, the National Board engineers had packed their suitcases, moved on, and were busily inspecting another city. So swiftly did this municipal survey work progress that as early as October 1905, within one year of the Baltimore fire, an article in *World's Work* reported that as a result of thirty-two city inspections, such improvements as the following had already been made:

> In Pittsburgh, a new 6,000,000-gallon pumping station has been installed and a fire boat ordered; at Cincinnati the boilers of half a dozen engines have been overhauled; at Rochester a new fire alarm system has been installed and civil service introduced in the department; at Worcester new engines have been ordered. In every city of the thirty-two inspected, a reorganization of the fire service has followed.

Meanwhile, the Executive Committee of the National Board had taken another step to cope with the menace of big urban conflagrations. It had appointed a Committee of Twenty, consisting of some of the most authoritative men in the insurance business, and charged it with the duty of defining the boundaries of the congested districts of all cities and preparing an insurance schedule for these high-risk central areas. It is one of the ironies of fate that by April 18, 1906, when an earthquake set off the great San Francisco fire, the engineering inspection program had not yet covered the city by the Golden Gate. Had it done so, perhaps San Francisco might have brought about sufficient improvement in its fire-fighting system to have prevented at least part of the damage that laid it low. Yet some months before the earthquake and fire the Committee of Twenty had surveyed the city. In the light of what happened later, the following words from its report showed that the insurance men fully understood how perilous the San Francisco situation was:

> While two of the five sections into which the congested value district is divided involve only a mild conflagration hazard within their own limits, they are badly exposed by the others, in which all the elements of the conflagration hazard are present to a marked degree. Not only is the hazard extreme within the congested value district, but it is augmented by the presence of a surrounding compact, great-height, large-area, frame-residence district itself unmanageable from a fire-fighting standpoint by reason of adverse conditions introduced by topography.
>
> In fact, San Francisco has violated all underwriting traditions and precedents by not burning up; that it has not done so is largely due to the vigilance of the fire department, which cannot be relied upon indefinitely to stave off the inevitable.

These words were written in October 1905. To the city's credit it should be known that the authorities took the report seriously and started to make some improvements—though too late. Within six months San Francisco no longer "violated all underwriting traditions and precedents," and had, indeed, largely burned up.

This shocking tragedy in California, the greatest single

disaster that America has suffered, was the final proving event by which the National Board of Fire Underwriters demonstrated that it had come fully of age. For this time the insurance industry was more soundly financed than before, thanks to the separate companies' accumulated reserves. In consequence, rumors of bankruptcy and default were by no means so widespread in 1906 as those that had swept through the beleaguered cities in the days of the Portland, Chicago and Boston conflagrations. Yet the magnitude of the ruin was vastly greater—the total loss, insured and uninsured, amounting to an estimated $350,000,000. No one will ever know exactly how much it was. It is known, however, that the loss to 243 insurance companies amounted to $175,508,530, represented by about 150,000 individual claims. The area burned was 3000 acres, or about 4.7 square miles, embracing 520 city blocks. Some 25,000 buildings were destroyed, of which 3000 were built of brick or stone and 22,000 of frame.

Summing up the experience a year later to the 1907 annual meeting, National Board President George W. Burchell expressed in these words the severity of the financial blow to the insurance business, and at the same time paid tribute to the way it had come through its most severe trial:

> The calamity was a shock to the business of the entire country and its severe test upon the insurance interests can only be appreciated by the companies themselves, yet it showed most of them to be strong enough to meet their obligations, and it is remarkable that so few of them were compelled to retire from business.
>
> After the Chicago fire over fifty joint stock Fire Insurance Companies went into liquidation, and many more after the Boston fire of the following year, whereas only twenty (and a number of these afterward resumed) are reported to have

suspended after the San Francisco fire notwithstanding the extent of the loss, amounting to a sum as large as the aggregate of all of the great conflagrations in the United States for the last fifty years . . .

This single conflagration swept away not only every dollar of profit previously made by the Companies out of underwriting since 1860, which is as far back as the National Board tables go, but cost them besides $79,708,174 for the period.

A host of heroic people toiled long and hard to help stricken San Francisco recover. Among them were public officials and common citizens, doctors, nurses, the volunteers in feeding stations, the soldiers under command of Generals Funston and Greely, and above all the skilled workmen who literally performed two years' work in one. Behind them, physically unseen yet quickly visible in its results, flowed a golden stream of fire insurance payments, pouring into the San Francisco area for months on end as claims were met and funds advanced. This money helped the city quickly rebuild and rise to new and glorious heights as the metropolis of the Pacific Coast.

After San Francisco, the National Board was to pass through a number of difficult times, each requiring its leaders to summon their energies and to exercise their best ingenuity in meeting new problems. No single event, however, struck with the sudden, devastating power of the 1906 earthquake and fire, or thrust upon the National Board at one moment a challenge of such proportions. The tests of later years, therefore, were accepted by a mature organization that had, quite literally, come through not only its baptism of fire, but also numerous proving ordeals. In the decade preceding World War I it emerged from them hardened and purified, in a sense, and dedicated to that public service which has remained its constant goal through subsequent years.

But the National Board of Fire Underwriters has been far from a static organization. Its responsibilities and concerns have changed and expanded with the needs of a rapidly developing American society. In both world wars, as well as during the Korean conflict, it has put its resources at the disposal of the United States Government, and assisted in many practical ways to protect the nation's military installations and production plants from accidental and sabotage fires. During the long, deep depression of the 1930s the National Board stood guard against the moral risks inevitable in times of bad business, and mobilized to fight arson as never before. And it has come through wave upon wave of legislative investigation and regulation, untarnished and in sound financial health.

As Americans in recent years have sought protection against a variety of perils other than fire, the basic fire insurance coverage has been steadily expanded to include such risks as hail, windstorm, earthquake, theft, explosion, falling aircraft, damage by automobile, and many more. Step by step the old fire policy has been transformed into a many-sided insurance policy protecting the holder against new dangers to which he has become exposed in a crowded, speeded-up, urbanized, electrified civilization that floats on a sea of flammable petroleum products. And the services of the National Board of Fire Underwriters, both to its member companies and to policyholders, have been amended and added to in order to keep up with these changes in our American way of life.

Many millions of people benefiting from these services are totally unaware that they are being performed. A description of what they are, how the National Board carries them out and why, and the way they came into being, is the substance of the chapters that follow.

IV

FINDING SAFETY IN STATISTICS

ON A SHORT, NARROW STREET in lower Manhattan Island slanting downhill from Broadway to the East River stands an inconspicuous building of red brick that is easily lost among its towering neighbors. Number Eighty-five John Street looks like just another office structure in the teeming financial district of New York, where waves of hurrying people crowd automobiles from the streets. But appearances are deceiving, because 85 John Street houses an institution unlike any other in the world. It is truly and literally unique—one of a kind.

This fourteen-floor building, headquarters of the National Board of Fire Underwriters since 1926, is the command post of a nationwide force that wages a ceaseless and largely unseen war against fire, the most costly and deadly menace to the property and lives of everyone in the United States. The public generally may not know it. The man who pays out hundreds, even thousands, of dollars each year in fire insurance may not recognize the extent of its protective influence. Yet the men and women at work in the National Board of Fire Underwriters Building are on the job not only to protect him from the danger of fire, explosion, and other hazards, but also to make possible the prompt payment of indemnity when catastrophe strikes.

The National Board's program of activity, evolved through many years since its impromptu start in 1866, can be summarized as fulfilling these two main purposes: first, preventing the outbreak of fire and reducing fire losses to the lowest possible level; second, aiding the victim of fire and other insured perils to get back to normal. Laboring patiently, in painstaking detail and without fanfare, seeking only to serve the public through serving the property insurance industry, the National Board of Fire Underwriters in 1966 achieves its centennial year. Everyone connected with it is proud of its long record of accomplishment. Yet all are aware, as well, of its many unfinished tasks that stretch out ahead as far as any man can foresee.

In a formal sense, the National Board of Fire Underwriters is a nationwide, educational, engineering, fact-finding service organization now maintained by approximately 200 capital stock insurance companies. Insurance policies issued by National Board member companies are held by people in every city and town, and nearly every crossroads village, in the United States. The purpose of the National Board is to provide to the insurance business those services that member companies either cannot provide alone, or cannot furnish to the same degree of thoroughness and efficiency by themselves. By pooling the information, the skills and the experience of the industry into a joint effort for the common benefit, while remaining competitive, the member companies have made possible what has been termed in the insurance business "the service beyond." That is, they provide service to the policyholder going beyond the terms of the insurance contract.

This "service beyond" of the National Board of Fire Underwriters has become the priceless ingredient in what the insurance business has to offer the American people. It increases the value of every policy written by member companies by an incalculable amount.

While the "service beyond" aids all policyholders, the work of the National Board in fire and loss prevention by its very nature benefits everyone in the country, whether insured or not. Fire out of control has no respect for the dividing line between insured and uninsured property. The National Board's program of services is paid for indirectly by the policyholders of member companies. Yet if its activities were allocated to the entire American nation, the real beneficiary, the cost would amount to *less than 3¢ per person per year.* In almost no other way do so many benefit so much for so little.

To gain an impression of the way the National Board goes about its work one is led logically to the executive offices on the twelfth floor of the John Street building. Here is its nerve center, so to speak, where the activity of the association's permanent staff is put in motion and maintained according to policies set by National Board committees. These committees are really the mainsprings of all National Board activities.

Some national trade associations are leader-oriented, reflecting the personality of one dominant figure who runs the organization largely as if it were his own show. Other groups are staff-oriented; in them the determining voice in their affairs comes from a team of key staff employees who have gained special knowledge of the association program through years of experience at its national center. The National Board of Fire Underwriters, in contrast, is a committee-oriented organization.

Important developments of National Board policy come from standing committees composed of leading executives of the member companies. In fact, the companies assign their best men to National Board work, and it is not at all uncommon to see a committee meeting that brings together a number of company presidents, leading officers and outstanding department heads. Through the committees on which these men serve they determine National Board policies and set up projects in support of them to be carried out by the staff employees of the National Board. The committees meet in the twelfth-floor board room, for the most part. They report at regular intervals to the Executive Committee of the National Board, as well as to the annual meeting, which brings together, each spring, several hundred officers of the member companies to review the year's work.

The staff, in its turn, reports to those National Board committees responsible for the part of the total program that is the special domain of each. Thus, it comes about that each of the major divisions of the staff is closely tied to a parent committee with the same, or a similar, name. For example, the National Board's Actuarial Bureau reports to the Actuarial Bureau Committee, the Engineering Department to the Committee on Engineering, and the legal staff to the Committee on Laws. The headquarters staff acts as the day-to-day executive arm of the National Board committees, which are really the heart of the organization.

An association with such a broad range of interests that is run largely by committees might easily find itself working inefficiently or at cross purposes were it not held together by a central force. Coordinator of the entire National Board structure is its general manager, Lewis A. Vincent, the executive officer. By the fact that he attends all standing committee meetings as ex officio secretary, the general manager is the central figure of the organization, in the sense that he keeps in close personal touch with all its activities. Being a veteran in National Board service, he brings continuity through the years to its program, as committee members come and go. Because of his central position he can advise every responsible person in the National Board as to what others are doing. Thus, he acts as the liaison between all its disparate parts. It is his duty to see that the program of the organization is executed by the staff. His lines of responsibility lead outward to the member companies by way of the National Board committees and the annual meeting. They also lead inward to the six principal departments or bureaus. All told, the National Board staff numbers close to 400, about three-fourths of them being in the New York office and most of the others being in the Chicago and San Francisco regional offices.

Such, in brief, is the structure of the National Board and its method of operation. Have they been effective in practice? Has the National Board of Fire Underwriters, in the long view of its history, justified the thought, work and money that have gone into it since 1866?

In 1964 an estimated one and one-half billion dollars' worth of property in the United States was destroyed by fire. Roughly another billion dollars' worth of destruction was caused by wind, hail, explosion and related hazards. In addition close to 12,000 lives were claimed by the tragedy of fire. Both figures set new records in the dollar value of loss suffered by American property owners within a year.

But loss totals expressed in dollars of value do not tell the full story. Ours is a dynamic, expanding economy, with more industries, houses and other things of value exposed to these risks each year than in the year before. The record shows, without a doubt, that despite the steady increase in fire and related losses over the years since estimates were first made, the value of all property subject to these risks has increased more rapidly than the loss figures. In other words, America has been making progress in the continuing war against fire losses. Since World War II, in fact, the values that might have been burned or otherwise damaged have increased at a pace one and one-half times that of the fire-loss rate.

Since the turn of the century measurable progress has been made in the control of fire waste. The ratio of fire loss to national wealth, in terms of things that can burn (burnable property), has been reduced by two-thirds. The toll of lives lost due to fire is another yardstick. In 1953 about 12,000 lives were taken by fire. At that time the population of the country was about 157,000,000. In 1964 the population reached 190,000,000 and the death toll was 11,800.

There is, of course, no room for complacency. But the relative progress that has been made clearly justifies the years of effort by everyone involved in the campaign for a safer, more secure way of life. In this campaign the National Board has long played a noteworthy part, in keeping with the highest ideals of good citizenship.

All insurance is based on the calculation of probabilities. The only way in which we can reckon the probability of future events is to study the record of the past and project its lessons into the period ahead. Keeping the record, analyzing it and projecting from it are the work of the professional known as the actuary.

The title "actuary" stems originally from the Latin *actuarius*. In ancient Rome, the *actuarius* was a clerk who recorded the events, or acts, of his day. Like him, the modern insurance actuary compiles the record of those events that are meaningful to the writing of soundly based insurance. To do so, he must recognize the essential so that it can be extracted from a mass of happenings. If his methods are well conceived and accurately pursued, his statistics can guide engineers and others to the causes of fires. Today's actuary is much more than merely the recorder of what *has* happened. He is also mathematician, analyst, and collector of vital intelligence.

Just as the work of the individual actuary is the center of the insurance business, so the work of the Actuarial Bureau has been essential to the National Board of Fire Underwriters. The bureau fills dual functions. On the one hand, it is a central pool for collecting information on losses paid by member companies, collating the data and reporting them to agencies of state governments. This was the bureau's original purpose when it was set up a half century ago; today it is designated as the official statistical agency for nearly all the fifty states. But the Actuarial Bureau also provides the means whereby the causes of fires and other losses can be tabulated and the results studied by the engineers, to the end that hazards can be reduced and American lives and property can be protected.

The first function meets the needs of the insurance business to inform state regulatory agencies of their loss experience, broken down by classifications of risk, so that the regulation of rates can be based on the actual facts. The second function meets society's need to know the cause of losses. Neither could be performed so well, if at all, without this cooperative pool of facts and figures. Indeed, it was the sheer impracticality and the cost of hundreds of companies facing the prospect of each supplying its own data to many states separately that led to the formation of the Actuarial Bureau. The money that would have been wasted by states and companies doing this multiple work would have come eventually from the pockets of the public. Merely by being in existence, therefore, the Actuarial Bureau illustrates the close intertwining of the private business and the public interest aspects of National Board work—so close, in fact, that they cannot be separated.

Information reaches the Actuarial Bureau, in the main, through three channels: the loss reports filed by insurance adjusters, questionnaires filled out by fire chiefs in communities of 2500 population and over, and insurance company reports of losses paid yearly, broken down by states and by class of risk.

By collecting, collating and analyzing these incoming data on a continuing national scale, the Actuarial Bureau is able to produce each year a unique and valuable series of reports on the fire and allied loss experience of the American people. These reports are at the same time sweepingly comprehensive and minutely detailed. In fact, when one appreciates the nature of its services, one cannot imagine how the insurance business could get along in today's world without the Actuarial Bureau. If it were not there, something else would have to be created to fulfill its function.

Tabulating the company reports on their dollar losses from fire and other perils each year is the activity that requires most of the Actuarial Bureau's time and man power. But of more direct interest to the public, as well as to fire departments and municipal government officials, are some of the other projects of tabulation and analysis. One of these is the statistical tabulation, directly from copies of the adjusters' loss reports, of known *causes* of fires, which the bureau performs for the National Board's Committee on Statistics and Origin of Losses. Since January 1, 1953, the Actuarial Bureau has been compiling two sets of figures on each fire. The first involves the source of the fire; the second relates to the substance ignited.

A carelessly thrown cigarette or an electrical short circuit would be put down as the source or cause of ignition. On the other hand, grease in a flue or wood shavings on the floor of a shop would be listed as the material ignited. Both are meaningful to the engineers studying the origin of fires with a view to curbing them, and often one is not much help without the other. By careful study of the Actuarial Bureau reports on fire causes, engineers, managers, and others in authority can draw the most practical conclusions on where to concentrate their fire-prevention efforts. In one case they might recommend a "No Smoking" rule when certain materials are present. In another, they might call for special precautions in a wooden shed, or clothing factory, or garage, when workmen are handling open lights, welding torches or tools that throw sparks.

The Actuarial Bureau compiles its figures on the origin of fires directly from the thousands upon thousands of adjusters' reports that flow into its big filing room in the John Street building. Some reports from adjusters understandably do not contain a cause of ignition, because this is not always known. But of those where the cause has been listed over a ten-year period since January 1, 1953, the category "matches and smoking" heads the list, being cited in 22.5 per cent of all the claims tallied. Electricity and electrical equipment, not including lightning, are the second most frequent known cause of fires leading to insurance claims, accounting for 20.7 per cent of the total. Fourteen other causes of ignition are listed, ranging from open flames and sparks to lightning, overheated flues, and spontaneous ignition, down to firecrackers and hot exhaust from internal-combustion engines.

According to the Actuarial Bureau tally, lightning has caused a number of losses that may surprise the typical city dweller—12.1 per cent of the ten-year total. Lightning losses are considered under the heading of "ignition," even though not all lightning strikes result in fires. Partly for this reason, and because lightning more often strikes trees than buildings, property losses from lightning have amounted to only 5.4 per cent of the total in dollar value. Quite the opposite is the case with fires originating from electricity and electrical equipment, because electrical fires often get a long, destructive head start before they are detected. Such fires accounted for 33.5 per cent of the dollar value lost, although they represented but 20.7 per cent of the number of fires.

The same is true of three of the less frequent fire causes: spontaneous ignition, incendiarism and vandalism, and welding torches. These three categories combined represented but 3.5 per cent of all fires in the ten-year tally of the Actuarial Bureau, yet they caused 9.4 per cent of the value burned.

Statistical reports of this kind contain many lessons for those with the responsibility and the earnest desire to apply them. One obvious conclusion, of course, is that the careless smoker who does not pay proper attention to his smouldering cigarette butt or match is still a great public menace, despite all the campaigns of public education that have been directed at him and all the supposedly foolproof ash trays that manufacturers have turned out. Not counting small fires producing claims of less than $250 each (which the Actuarial Bureau does not include in its reports), matches and smoking have been the cause of a half million fires recorded by the bureau in the past ten years, on which the average insurance payment amounted to nearly $1400.

The record shows that Americans are as careless with electricity as they are with matches and smoking. When one considers that nearly 460,000 fires in the past ten years have been of known electrical origin, and that they have caused an average loss of more than $3300 each, it is easy to see that we have a long way to go before we can claim to have learned how to use electricity with an adequate degree of safety. To the extent that the Actuarial Bureau reports on the causes of ignition highlight such deficiencies, they tell a story that the public and the authorities should heed.

Exactly the same thing holds true for the second part of the Actuarial Bureau's work on the origin of fires—that relating to the materials first ignited, and from which they often spread into big fires. It is probably not surprising that the material most frequently ignited, and also the one sustaining by far the greatest dollar loss, is combustible material used in buildings, such as wooden floors and walls, laths, sheathing, and timbering. The next most frequently ignited materials, in order, are: cloth and other fiber products, which would include household curtains and draperies; grease, fats and similar flammables, often ignited in kitchen fires; and furniture, particularly upholstered pieces that are set on fire as a result of carelessness with cigarettes.

Petroleum products and by-products have been ignited in only 6.5 per cent of the fires tallied in the ten-year Actuarial Bureau report. But when these substances catch fire they are highly destructive, for such fires caused nearly $295,000,000 in damage—or 14.3 per cent of the dollar value lost where the material ignited was known. A lesson for homeowners, which the National Board of Fire Underwriters repeats every year during the holiday season, is that Christmas trees can catch on fire, and frequently do. So far no one has yet found a method of extinguishing a Christmas tree fire, because once set alight, the dry, resinous needles roar into flame before the homeowner can hope to douse them with a chemical extinguisher or water. The National Board has repeatedly stressed the safety message that a tree should stand in water, to prevent the branches and needles from drying in a warm house. Nevertheless, claims above the discounted minimum ($250 or less) have been recorded in nearly 2700 instances of Christmas tree fires, and the average of these claims has been $1400. These figures alone carry a message to celebrants of a joyous holiday who would avoid having the festivity of Christmas turn to tragedy by fire.

In its role as combined record keeper and analyst for all those forces in American society involved in the war against fire waste, the Actuarial Bureau carries on a number of other statistical studies that are highly useful in planning fire-prevention strategy. One of these is its work in evaluating the outstanding factors that have contributed to permitting certain fires to become large losses, amounting to $100,000 or more each. In releasing its latest accumulation of information on large-loss fires, furnished to the National Board by insurance boards and bureaus throughout the country, the Committee on Statistics and Origin of Losses reported in May 1964:

> The contents of this table are particularly recommended for study by those having responsibility relating to the planning, maintenance, and inspection of buildings as well as those in the fields of fire prevention and education.

The committee cited the following factors as the most frequent ones contributing to large-loss fires over the previous ten-year period. The percentages indicate the frequence of occurrence of these factors (often more than one in a given fire) related to the total number of large-loss fires:

Highly combustible contents	64.0%
Delayed discovery—fire detected by outsiders, police or other persons not connected with risk	54.7%
Building heavily involved upon arrival of first-alarm response apparatus	37.6%
Building and structures having large undivided areas	36.9%
Highly combustible interior construction and finish	32.1%
Roof collapse interfered with fire fighting	31.4%
Water supply inadequacy or failure	31.4%

As in its other studies, the Actuarial Bureau in this analysis points the finger at certain places where thought and effort can well be expended to reduce such large losses. Among them one can list the installation of automatic sprinklers and fire alarms, the importance of fire resistive construction, and the maintenance of an adequate water supply.

From its other continuing studies by which the Actuarial Bureau is constantly keeping its eye on fire losses, the better to combat them, these conclusions have emerged:

Total fire losses in the United States, both insured and uninsured, rose to an estimated $1,405,558,000 in 1963, a figure 11 per cent above the previous year and a new high mark in fire destruction. It has been pointed out at the same time, however, that since World War II the total national wealth subject to fire destruction, expressed in dollar value, has been rising more rapidly than fire loss. In this relative respect, then, the struggle to control fire destruction has been successful, even though the absolute loss in dollars has been steadily increasing.

Breaking down the estimated total fire losses by months, the Actuarial Bureau has found that the period of heaviest losses is the winter, from December through March, the peak loss month being January. On the other hand, the lightest losses have occurred from August to November, with the lowest loss rate falling in September.

Another slant on the national fire toll is obtained from annual reports on the number of fires which cooperating fire chiefs in about 2800 communities of 2500 or more inhabitants submit annually to the Actuarial Bureau. Taken together, these indicate the frequency of fires and the kind of fires that have occurred. Because they include all fires within the communities whose chiefs report, they therefore embrace fires where the losses are not insured by National Board members. The following are some of the conclusions that stand out from the 1963 summary of these fire chiefs' reports to the Actuarial Bureau:

Nearly 60 per cent of all reported alarms involved non-building fires, and just over 40 per cent involved buildings.

Roughly 70 per cent of all building fires occurred in residences.

There were markedly fewer fires per thousand population in cities of more than 100,000 residents than in smaller cities. This was true both of building and of non-building fires.

Record keeping and analyses such as these have by no means provided the ultimate weapons for conquering the menace of fire to civilized society. But as the National Board each year learns more about what causes fires to break out, where they occur and when, and what enables them to spread, the insurance industry is better equipped to help everyone find the most important points to attack.

Through this kind of continuing study, hopefully, the coming years may witness a steady refinement in fire-prevention and fire-fighting techniques.

There is quite another element in the study of the why, where, and when of fire losses, and it, too, falls within the Actuarial Bureau's field of responsibility. This is the human element. Keeping the record of *whose* property has burned is of continuing interest to the underwriters, and has been since well before the National Board, in 1866, resolved in its original statement of purpose:

> To repress incendiarism and arson by combining in suitable measures for the apprehension, conviction, and punishment of criminals engaged in this nefarious business.

The starting point for the human, or personal, side of the national fire-loss record is the preparation, by the adjuster who handles a claim, of what is commonly known in the business as the Confidential Adjuster's Loss Report. In most states the adjuster makes this report on all losses of $100 or more, discounting the lesser ones. One copy is sent directly to the Actuarial Bureau, where clerks extract the vital information from it and prepare two index cards —one according to the assured's name and one according to the location of the risk. The two cards are filed respectively in a name file and a geographical file.

Altogether the Actuarial Bureau maintains a collection of about 6,000,000 such cards, each carrying the name of the assured, the town, county and state where the insured property is located, the date of the fire, amount of settlement and cause of the fire, if known. These index cards fill row upon row of file cabinets. Were they all placed in one continuous sequence they would require a card drawer well over one mile in length. And yet an Actuarial Bureau clerk can locate a given fire loss or search out a particular name, should a member company request it, within a minute or less.

One of the first questions on which an insurance company may want information is whether an applicant for a policy has any kind of past fire record. A query to the Actuarial Bureau will often elicit a swift reply from the Loss Record Index that the prospect has no record of fire losses at all. On the other hand, the company may be told that the LRI contains a record of his having suffered several fire losses within the past few years. In such a case the company may reconsider writing this particular risk.

Because *all* reported fire losses from member companies go into the Loss Record Index, there is nothing damaging to an individual in the fact that a memorandum of his claim is included among the other 6,000,000 entries. But a cumulative record of repeated losses may indicate to a prospective insurer that he should be careful. It may turn out that the individual is a habitually careless smoker, who has repeatedly fallen asleep leaving a lighted cigarette to cause fire damage to his home. Or it may show that a businessman has had so many small fires on his premises that underwriters can fairly conclude that he makes no real effort at fire prevention in his place of business.

Whatever the facts, or the inferences that underwriters may severally draw from the factual record, the Loss Record Index serves as a central collection point for information on what individuals were insured when fire struck. Like many other services of the National Board of Fire Underwriters, the Loss Record Index is a cooperative activity that it would be impossible for individual companies to compile and maintain on their own. And while member companies are the only ones privileged to obtain reports from the index, to the extent that it contributes to the constant war against fraud fires, set deliberately for criminal motives, it protects the lives and property of everyone else who might be injured by a fraud fire. In addition, this service helps to restrict the total losses of individuals who can be classed as "fire prone," and in this way acts to keep down insurance rates.

In order to keep the LRI current, old cards are removed from the files after eight years. About 300,000 reports come into the Actuarial Bureau yearly, although the number of fires they represent is somewhat lower. This is so because on occasion there are two or more reports on one fire, there being more than one company involved in the case.

The 6,000,000 cards in the Loss Record Index contain the total picture of all fire-loss claims that the assured have brought in the past eight years to companies that are members of the Actuarial Bureau. Interfiled with it is a much smaller collection of very special interest to the underwriters—that of the Loss Information Service (LIS). The National Board describes this latter index as one "of those individuals and corporations having a fire history of interest to underwriting and loss departments." In plain English, the LIS is an index of persons and businesses that have been connected with suspicious fires and proven fraud fires, filed by name, as well as by "case"—each suspicious fire being given a case number. The supporting data, including reports from adjusters and investigators, are filed under the given case. The files contain about 150,000 index cards, which because of cross-filing represent a somewhat smaller number of active cases—perhaps 115,000 to 120,000.

A card enters the Loss Information Service file in any of a number of ways, although it usually starts with the insurance adjuster's report. After a fire, the adjuster is asked to state whether he recommends the continuation of a policy; he may say, "No." This negative reply is a flag to the LIS, which queries the adjuster by letter or telephone asking his reasons. His answer may lead to filing an LIS card, or it may not, depending on the circumstances. If the evidence seems to warrant it, the LIS will call on the Arson, Theft and Fraud Department of the National Board to send an agent to make inquiries, develop the facts, and submit a report. All this may convince the Arson Department to take a second look at a past loss incurred by the same assured, one which hitherto had seemed quite legitimate.

The entire purpose of the Loss Information Service is to provide the underwriters with an exchange of information that helps them suppress arson to defraud. Founded at the end of World War I, at the same time that the National Board set up the Loss Record Index, the Loss Information Service proved its great value almost at once. Now it receives approximately 13,000 requests each year from companies asking for reports on prospective policyholders.

When a company finds that a most desirable piece of business is in prospect with a Mr. X, but finds that man's name in its LIS card file, it will not necessarily conclude that the insurance should not be written. The procedure to be followed is for an authorized representative of the company to submit an inquiry form, which he must sign personally, to the Actuarial Bureau of the National Board of Fire Underwriters, asking for the information on which the LIS card is based. The LIS in reply sends back a one-page summary of the information in the LIS files, sticking closely to the known facts. It does not attempt to influence the company, and recognizes it is not in the Actuarial Bureau's province to do so.

The company, of course, is perfectly free to write the business or not, as it pleases. And frequently companies will write policies covering individuals whose names are in the LIS index, without even submitting an inquiry. In fact, there is a wide variance now in the use of the service between companies. And the interest in consulting LIS over prospective business has varied widely according to the temper of the times. In the 1930s, when depression conditions made people conservative about undertaking risks and pessimistic about any kind of business venture, companies sent in many more inquiries for LIS service than in the prosperous 1950s and the 1960s. In fact, some ninety people were needed to operate the service in depression times, in contrast to about thirty at present. And for all the bad-risk individuals that member companies have been able to keep off their books by resorting to the Loss Information Service, there must be many others, no one can say how many, who decided against trying to defraud a fire insurance company out of respect for its intelligence system. Every honest policyholder was thereby the gainer.

Most of the work of gathering information on suspected and proven cases of arson for fraud falls to the National Board's Arson, Theft and Fraud Department. Quite naturally this investigating unit of the National Board maintains close contact with LIS so that the latter, which is at heart a record-maintaining unit, can report to the members, when requested, what the investigators have learned. The "when requested" is important, because LIS files are kept strictly confidential. No one below the rank of an executive officer of a member company, or an employee designated by him to make such inquiries, will be furnished an LIS report on any prospective policyholder.

Nor do all "suspicious fires" turn out as they may seem at first, and the underwriters, the LIS and the Arson Department are all aware of this. Not long ago the LIS staff was disturbed over a seemingly contradictory report from the West Coast concerning a prominent figure of impeccable reputation. Within a short time this man had suffered a number of fires at his home that bore all the markings of having been deliberately set. Yet his entire character and record were at variance with the usual fraud-fire type. In the files his case was flagged with an identifying mark that means "under investigation." Meanwhile, National Board people who knew about the matter were deeply puzzled. When the affair was finally cleared up, it turned out that the upright citizen's property had actually been set afire, as suspected, but there had been no intent to defraud the insurance companies. The arson was the work of a disgruntled employee who sought to get even with his boss by setting his property afire.

In the years just after the San Francisco earthquake and fire the states began to require an increasing number of reports from each company doing business within the state. To the companies, the burden of supplying them became excessively heavy, because there was no uniformity among the state requirements, either in the time period to be covered or in the form in which the report was demanded. In 1912 the Superintendent of Insurance of New York asked for a detailed record of every company's experience in the state during the preceding twelve years. The record was to include the dollar value of premiums collected and the value of claims paid in each classification of risk, such as bakeries, hotels, frame dwellings, or whatever classes the companies used. The National Board then set up a committee to consider how to carry out such a huge and burdensome job most effectively and so save everyone the waste of duplicated work.

In 1913 the annual convention of the state insurance

commissioners discussed the wisdom of adopting one standard report form, and in response the National Board the next year set up a permanent Actuarial Bureau Committee to work out the details. Little time was lost, and starting from January 1, 1915, the Actuarial Bureau began to compile fire-loss statistics on a uniform plan that would serve both the commissioners and the companies in the most economical way, and on the broadest, and therefore most statistically valuable, scale.

Before the Actuarial Bureau went into operation in 1915 each company had collected its own figures on fire losses by any means that came to hand. Reliable, broadly based statistics had never been compiled by any agency. As to rating property to be insured, the leading figures in each company had their own pet ideas on how they should classify risks. It was a system of rating, if it can be called that, based on only partial knowledge, with a large element of individual hunch involved. Actual experience—the precise record of fire losses by class of risk—played a very small part in rate setting because there was no agency compiling data and keeping records on a large scale. No one, therefore, really knew whether bakeries had proved to be better fire risks over the years than restaurants, or whether lumberyards, for instance, were as good risks as boat yards.

It was against this background that Ellis G. Richards of the North British and Mercantile, then vice president of the National Board, proposed the appointment of the Actuarial Bureau Committee in 1914. At about the same time Richards developed his own fire risk classification system, which the Actuarial Bureau adopted upon opening up for business in 1915. It was soon found, however, that in his effort to pinpoint each class of risk Richards had cut the field into bits that were too fine. His system provided for 584 classes of occupancy, some of which were too limited in scope to produce useful figures. In the following decades several other classification systems were tried, then discarded in favor of new ones. The present plan, embracing 115 classes of risk, was put into effect in 1947.

These classes are each made up of properties and activities showing a common degree of risk through years of actuarial study, even though the kinds of activity within each class may have little connection with one another. The classes vary widely in size and in dollar value covered. One that embraces patent-leather manufacturing, for instance, represents less than $30,000 in yearly premiums paid to National Board companies. That covering tobacco factories accounts for only about $60,000 in premiums. At the other end of the scale the class embracing oil refineries and similar risks covers more than $12,000,000, and the light metalworking class, $28,000,000. Some $67,000,000 is paid yearly to insure the farm property class, and $164,000,000 is paid annually to insure dwellings, not including their contents. National totals are, of course, higher than these figures because not all premiums paid in the United States are collected by companies that are National Board members.

In order to compile what it terms its Composite Classified Underwriting Experience report, the Actuarial Bureau each year receives close to 3,500,000 punched cards from the insurance companies. The collecting and sorting takes place in a large room that fills most of the rear half of the tenth floor in the National Board building at 85 John Street, New York. Here the cards flow for weeks through a series of sorting and tabulating machines. From the tabulators emerge a series of annual reports covering the detailed fire and extended coverage experience for the past year in each of the fifty states and the District of Columbia, together with totals for the United States. There is also a summary relating the experience of the entire United States in the past year to that of the four preceding years.

It is a tremendous task for the companies to compile the data in this form since they must prepare 30,000 or more punched cards apiece, on the average, and in the case of the biggest companies, considerably more. But the trouble of supplying the Actuarial Bureau with the information is a minor price the company pays for the far greater amount of information it receives in return. When the year's figures are all compiled, each member company gets back a complete set of reports showing how all companies together fared during the past year in every particular on which it filed a report of its own experience. Thus, the Actuarial Bureau acts as a great cooperative pool of information, to which each contributes its own part, and from which each receives the total picture.

From its beginning the Actuarial Bureau has supplied copies of its underwriting experience reports to state insurance departments, or commissions. In serving these regulatory agencies of the states, the Actuarial Bureau is directly serving the public. The insurance departments of the several states have the legal duty to protect the public interest, and the Actuarial Bureau serves as the instrument through which they obtain the facts. At present, insurance authorities in all but four states have named the Actuarial Bureau as their official statistical agency, and rely on its compilations as the official record of experience in fire, homeowners, farm owners and certain other lines of insurance. Thus, the Actuarial Bureau is carrying on an essential quasi-public function as a natural byproduct of its work in behalf of the insurance industry.

The Composite Classified Underwriting Experience reports include losses from perils other than fire, but these are carried in less detail. Among them are windstorm and hail, leakage from sprinklers, radioactive contamination, earthquake, and damage from aircraft and vehicles. While there has been a tendency in recent years toward insurance against several of these perils in addition to fire, the principal form of property insurance remains protection against fire loss. The day may come when another peril will supersede fire as the primary danger to property, but it is not yet in sight.

Most of each classified experience report is devoted to insured fire losses. The dollar values of premiums written during the year, the losses paid, and the consequent loss ratio are detailed under each of the 115 classes of risk, which are determined, as noted earlier, by the degree of risk involved. It is also important to take into consideration the material of which a structure is built, as well as its accessibility to a responsible fire-fighting organization. For each class of risk, therefore, the Actuarial Bureau divides insured properties into three groups according to their construction. These are frame (wood), brick (which includes other building stone), and fire resistive, a term meaning that the property has a steel or reinforced concrete frame. There are minor differences from state to state in the interpretation of cases that fall somewhere on the border line between these structural groups.

In addition, an insured property is rated as "protected" if it lies within the area of responsibility of a fire company that meets certain minimal standards in equipment, manning and water supply; otherwise it is "unprotected," meaning that it does not enjoy effective coverage by a fire company.

A classified experience report subdivides each class of

risk in a given state into six groups, according to kind of structure and access to protection by a fire department. By studying this experience compiled by the Actuarial Bureau, state insurance department officials can gauge the loss record in their own state against that of the country as a whole. Without this work of the Actuarial Bureau, no one would have such a picture. The classified underwriting experience reports provide the state departments, and, through them, the American people, with the record of past losses essential to setting rates fair both to the public and to the underwriters.

So goes the work of the Actuarial Bureau—from the sweeping generalities of the nationwide loss ratio to the particular details of one policyholder whose losses are under scrutiny. Only an organization with the facilities of the National Board of Fire Underwriters could carry out a program of documentation and analysis that puts the national experience, so to speak, within the field of both the telescope and the microscope. Although fire waste is a national problem, no other agency is so well equipped to address it on a national scale. Thus it has come about, and the work of the Actuarial Bureau illustrates the services of the National Board most graphically, that this institution of private enterprise has adopted the public business in its own interest and that of the millions of people it serves.

V

THE ENDLESS WAR AGAINST ARSON

FROM ITS BEGINNING in 1866 the National Board of Fire Underwriters has been deeply concerned with the pursuit of those people who deliberately set property afire. At first the effort was almost exclusively directed toward the arsonist whose fire setting was actuated by criminal motives. In more recent times, however, with the development of a deeper understanding by the medical profession of abnormal psychology, the Arson, Theft and Fraud Department of the National Board has been concerned, as well, with mentally ill fire setters, who light fires under compulsions they cannot control. Both are the business of this department of the National Board because both are involved in determining how a particular fire started —or was started.

There are criminals for whom professional fire setting is a way of life, and the department is concerned with the apprehension of these dangerous enemies of society. By its nature their specialty, arson, is a stealthy crime done in secret. For that reason it is extremely difficult to prove beyond a reasonable doubt. Unlike many other crimes, the execution of it often destroys much of the evidence. A building fire that has a roaring start before the firemen arrive on the scene can easily consume all material evidence that it was set. One may be left with suspicions, but juries cannot convict on evidence that goes only as far as strengthening suspicion but not so far as proof. Largely for this reason, therefore, but also because the public generally does not recognize the arsonist as a dangerous menace to society, prosecutors find it more productive to spend their time pursuing other game.

It is the public's loss that this is so, because arson is an increasing danger, and not to insurance companies alone. Everyone in American society has an interest in the suppression of deliberate fire setting. A building fire endangers other property in the vicinity, and menaces the lives of those who may be caught in buildings to which the fire can spread. It exposes firemen to the danger of injury, and sometimes death. Further, every fire adds eventually to the cost of maintaining fire departments and to the cost of fire insurance. Every time, therefore, that the fire bell rings and the sirens scream, they sound a loss for everyone in the community, near or far. No one is uninvolved.

In the year ending April 30, 1964, the Arson, Theft and Fraud Department of the National Board completed 3860 investigations of questionable fire losses, about the same number of cases it had closed in each of the previous ten years. The department concluded that in 904 instances, 25 per cent of all cases, there was probable fraud. The term "probable fraud" means that the circumstances of the fire loss, taken as a whole, indicate to the Arson Department that its original questioning of a suspicious fire loss at the time the claim was made has been supported by its investigation, and that the department believes the fire was deliberately set in order to collect insurance on the loss. The case developed by the department may be strong enough to convince the underwriters to resist payment of the claim brought by the assured, or it may not. But this figure of 25 per cent conclusions of probable fraud among 3860 cases investigated in 1963–1964 set a new record.

The incidence of probable fraud has been climbing fast since the late 1950s, but before that it was very low. During a fifteen-year period, from 1941 through 1955, practically all incendiary fires in the United States were attributed to juveniles, mentally disturbed persons, vandals, thrill seekers, unlawful intruders or persons motivated by spite or a desire for revenge. The motive of defrauding insurance companies was encountered in a very small proportion of the cases investigated. The Annual Report of the National Board in 1946, for example, stated:

> Such fires as have had profit for a motive have been confined to cases where the circumstances were very unusual and have been very few in number. Reports from our Chicago office indicated only two fires during the year set for the purpose of collecting insurance.

Continuing good times during the postwar years, and the boost to the economy accompanying America's involvement in the Korean conflict of 1950–1953, tended to decrease the incidence of fires set for profit. Fire-for-hire criminals were not in the picture. The 1951 Annual Report contained this significant comment: "As has been the case for some years past, no evidence was found this year of organized arson rings nor of activities of professional fire bugs."

Things continued this way for several more years, during which the investigation work of the National Board centered on other forms of arson, such as fire setting by mischievous juveniles, by adults motivated by grudges, by pathological fire setters (pyromaniacs), thrill seekers, and others. Then, starting in 1955, the fraud element in incendiary fires became steadily more noticeable. Year by year it has increased, and by 1959 it became so marked that the department began to tabulate separately those fire losses in which the apparent motive for the fire setting was to defraud insurance companies. By 1961 staff members of the Arson, Theft, and Fraud Department were devoting practically all their time to the investigation of fraud fires. Member companies were warned of the reappearance on the national scene, for the first time since the depths of the depression, of professional arson rings. The 1961 Annual Report listed 740 probable fraud fires in more than 4000 closed cases. More recently the number of probable fraud fires rose successively to 780, to 875, and then to 904 in 1964.

At first glance these rising statistics of fraud fires might lead one to believe that the Arson Department has been losing the struggle against crime by burning. Or one might conclude that it has been discovering lately the kind of frauds that could have been present earlier, though undetected, in each year's fire losses. The truth is that objective conditions, economic and social, lying completely outside the fields of insurance and the National Board's areas of concern, have combined to cause more fraud fires in recent years than before 1955.

One factor, certainly, is the perilous health of many small businesses in times of easy credit, when the dominating spirit is that of swift pursuit of the "quick buck" and the "killing" by taking risks. As population in urban areas has rapidly expanded, entrepreneurs have fallen over themselves in the attempt to keep one jump ahead of city growth and anticipated public demand for a great variety of goods, services and amusements. Not surprisingly, thousands of poorly financed, overly optimistic plungers have gone into businesses for which they had no special aptitude or training, and found, after a while, they could not make a go of it. The record of small business failures, even in the postwar years of general prosperity, documents this phenomenon. And in their private capacities, too many individuals have bought and furnished homes that they could not pay for without a great financial strain. Conditions such as this, on a national scale, provide the background against which an insurance fire takes on a rosy glow in the mind's eye of the morally weak, desperate person who is burdened by debts. In such a situation the criminal element has turned to arson as a marketable service to be provided for a price.

The two elements, in fact, go hand in hand. Widespread failures in marginal small businesses have attracted hardened criminals to adding arson to their repertoire of shady services; and the criminal arsonist, in turn, has actively solicited business among those to whom his services are likely to have the strongest appeal.

The most desirable result of an investigation by the National Board's Arson Department is preventing a fraud fire's being touched off at all. But the opportunity to accomplish this comes all too rarely. It happens more often that the fraud fire actually occurs, and that arrests are made later as a result of the investigation of the loss. Frequently the person arrested is the assured, the policyholder who caused the fire to be touched off. Sometimes the police also catch the hired "torch," the person who actually set the fire for payment.

In most cases where the Arson Department concludes that a fire loss merits the label "probable fraud," but where no arrest is made, the investigation is by no means a loss of time and money. It may give the underwriters enough information to convince them that the fire was deliberately set to defraud, and so help them resist making the insurance payment. And even though the evidence may not be strong enough to induce the district attorney to seek the indictment for arson, it may be all the insurance company requires to make a winning argument in court if the assured sues to collect.

In rendering this service, the Arson, Theft and Fraud Department pays for itself many times over each year. For example, the 904 probable fraud losses in the year covered in the 1964 Annual Report involved insurance coverage totaling $36,500,000. Nearly two-thirds of this amount was written through companies that are members of the National Board. The 162 cases in which arrests were made involved insurance written through National Board companies totaling $3,750,000. It is safe to assume that in almost every case where arrests were made, the insuring companies did not pay claims. There is no tabulation of how many claims were dropped completely, or settled in compromise, by the assured in suspicious fires when they learned the extent of the arson evidence possessed by the underwriters and the local authorities.

To operate the Arson, Theft and Fraud Department for a year, the National Board appropriates $1,500,000, which is a small part of the money it saves the insurance industry. The bill is paid entirely by the member companies through their membership assessments. Indirectly, of course, the cost of the department's work is borne by millions of insured policyholders, at a price per person of a few cents a year. And if the cost of the National Board's ceaseless war against arson were allocated to the entire American public—for everyone is being served and protected whether he owns fire insurance or not—the per capita cost comes down to less than one cent per year.

The staff of the Arson Department numbers a little more than one hundred. The backbone and muscle of the organization are some ninety special agents, spread geographically so as to cover all fifty states. Headquarters clerical workers and supervisors in the main office in New York, and in regional National Board offices in Chicago and San Francisco, comprise the rest of the department. Each of the special agents is responsible for a territory roughly the size of a state, or a half state in some cases. Many fires in the biggest cities, such as New York, Los Angeles and Philadelphia, are not investigated by the National Board, however, because in those cities the fire and police departments are staffed with their own experienced arson detectives.

The typical Arson Department special agent is a mature man who has been through considerably more training than the average law enforcement officer, and who has proved himself in investigative work before he is hired by the National Board. The manager of the Arson, Theft and Fraud Department is a former special agent of the Federal Bureau of Investigation, and about half the men in his department are FBI alumni. Others have joined the National Board staff after long service with big city police departments, the state police, the Federal Narcotics Bureau or other law enforcement agencies. The vast majority have undergone special training as detectives, and have held the rank of inspector, police lieutenant and sometimes captain. Among them are law school graduates, linguists, and certified public accountants.

In the field, that is, the area where he lives and works, the National Board special agent is almost entirely on his own. He makes his own schedule but his work is recorded on the daily report he makes to his superior. He works out of his home, and travels where he is needed in his own car. Within his area of responsibility it is the special agent's job to develop his contacts with the local police and fire department heads in such a way that they look upon him as a colleague to whom they can turn for assistance. Frequently they will invite him to join them in investigating a fire that has aroused their suspicions. The special agent also keeps in close touch with the insurance adjusters in his territory, for the same reason. In many instances the adjuster will call upon him, with a request that the special agent inquire into a fire loss because he has reason to believe that the facts of a claim are not exactly as represented by the assured. Or the special agent may be called upon by the police or fire department while the flames are still mounting, because the fire is so obviously of incendiary origin.

But whenever he investigates a fire loss, the special agent's purpose is to put himself at the disposal of the public authorities, because his mission is to help them to determine how a fire started. In many cases he is far more of a specialist in this work than anyone else present, and this is particularly true in the smaller communities. He has been through literally hundreds of such investigations, whereas those who call on him may have had little or no fire investigation experience. Yet the Arson Department special agent always remains a friendly assistant; he never forgets that he has been invited to participate in that role. He keeps away from publicity, and whatever his part in solving a case of suspected arson, he sees that the credit is not diverted from the agency conducting the investigation.

The first-class arson investigator must possess a combination of qualities and abilities that makes his a most difficult specialty to master. First, of course, he must know all the tricks of fire setting to which the arsonist may resort. He must likewise be familiar with the art of fire fighting, and should know the physics and chemistry involved in both. He must be a detective with a "nose" or instinct for the few significant facts amid a jumble of many; yet he must also be a patient investigator of details who will conscientiously follow every clue to its end. He must be personable, so that he can secure the cheerful cooperation of those in authority. Yet he should be able to extract information from unwilling arson suspects and their accomplices by argument, by cajoling and, in some cases, by bluff. He must know the law of evidence and the rights of those whom he interrogates, and must respect with absolute scrupulousness the limits they may impose upon him. He must know enough about that part of abnormal psychology which concerns pyromania in order to recognize patterns of abnormal fire setting. Finally, he must be articulate. The written reports on his investigations which he sends to the National Board must be clear and precise. When called upon as a trial witness he must offer testimony that conveys his meaning and his findings exactly. When invited to lecture at arson seminars and other educational meetings, he is expected to be a worthy representative of the National Board of Fire Underwriters.

To serve as a special agent in the Arson, Theft and Fraud Department, therefore, a man should be something out of the ordinary as an arson investigator. Yet the manager of the department does not have to hunt out candidates to fill vacancies on the staff; he has far more applicants than positions to fill, and he can be highly selective.

The first duty of the special agent in connection with any given fire loss is to see whether or not the fire was accidental. Most fires, of course, are accidents, although it must be said that a great many are owing to careless lack of precautions that almost invite accidents. Usually the fire fighters find clear evidence of the way a fire started, such as charring where the overloaded electric wire skirted the woodwork, or obvious signs corroborating the housewife's statement that she spilled cooking fat on the gas stove. If there are no suspicious circumstances to lead the fire chief to suspect the fire in any way, there is no reason to call in an arson investigator.

Any number of telltale signs, however, can alert the suspicions of the fire chief, the police, the insurance adjuster or the National Board's special agent. A few typical examples follow:

If a modern, fire-resistive building is burning furiously before the first piece of fire-fighting apparatus arrives, the size of the fire and the speed with which it spread initially cry out for explanation.

The appearance of separate fires at different points in a burning building, with no obvious connection between the distinct blazes, is too much of a coincidence to be disregarded.

Color and odor of the smoke can indicate the kind of material that is burning, and if observed in time can help isolate the substance on fire before the building itself is burning hard. Certain commonly used incendiary materials give off a black smoke, whereas others produce a heavy white smoke. Some give off characteristic odors while burning. If the burning material seems out of place, questions are in order.

The removal beforehand, under whatever pretext, of articles that normally would have been in the line of the fire is suspicious. They might include valuable pieces of furniture, expensive tools, items of sentimental value, pets, personal papers and, most notably, the fire insurance policy.

The condition of doors and windows may point to an effort to conceal a fire and impede entry to the building while the fire is gaining headway. Sometimes firemen arrive on the scene to find all doors and windows locked and shades drawn down tight when they are not usually in this position.

Bystanders and volunteers to assist who seem unusually interested in finding out how the fire started have proven over the years to include a large number of fire setters, of the pathological or thrill-seeker type.

The fire that appears to fit into a pattern of similar fires is by that fact suspicious, whether suffered by the same assured in close sequence or by people in the same neighborhood, or if they originated in the same manner, such as in street-level hallways accessible without a house key.

Finally, and most important in fraud fires, a fire merits close scrutiny if it is marked by questionable circumstances and it also follows closely upon the issuance of a fire insurance policy of large amount, or an increase in the value covered.

If any of these telltale signs of arson are present, an investigation of the fire is called for. It is at this point that good rapport between fire chief and the National Board representative in the area is most important, because the fire may have taken place in a town fifty miles from the special agent's home and he may not know about it until he is called upon by the chief to join in the investigation. It is National Board policy to respond to all requests for aid whenever the special agent's time permits, whether or not the loss involves a National Board of Fire Underwriters member company.

The investigation is officially conducted by the local agency (in some cities the fire department, in others the police), with the National Board representative helping in every possible way. But while he assists the local officials to sift the facts in order to get the truth about the fire, he at the same time has a primary duty to the National Board. This leads, at times, to his carrying his own investigation beyond the point where the local officials have satisfied their suspicions on a particular fire, because he may still be uneasy about it. And it is here that the special agent must exercise the utmost tact in working with the public authorities while also serving the association of which he is a staff representative. In most instances there is no conflict, because the local chiefs do not object to his carrying his own investigation beyond their stopping point.

The most important part of a fire investigation is the first inspection of the property by a trained arson specialist soon after the fire has been extinguished. Such an inspection is most fruitful if the blaze has been put out before most of the building is consumed, because a total-loss fire can destroy the material evidence of arson. On the other hand, when the fire fighters master the fire before the floor and walls are completely burned, the investigator has an excellent chance of finding evidence of exactly where and how the building caught fire.

If the National Board's special agent is present, he will accompany the city officials responsible and go with them through the building, or what is left of it, to determine the point of origin of the fire. They will interview the person who first discovered the fire (most often it is one person) and check his account of the starting point, if he observed the fire early, against the evidence they uncover inside the burned building.

The physical evidence often is found in the area of most heavy charring, at least in cases where enough remains to make such a determination. If the part most seriously damaged by charring is wood, the surface will be marked by what firemen term "alligatoring"—irregular cracking by lines that run in several directions, as on an alligator skin handbag, or on the surface of an old oil painting that has dried out. "Alligatoring" will not only help locate the point of origin of the fire, but it can also help determine whether there were two or more separate areas of burning, which may not have been seen before the smoke cleared. Charred floor areas leading away from the most heavily burned spot may indicate the presence of a flammable liquid that soaked into the wood floor and conducted the fire along the line of its flow. Unless there is a known reason why a flammable liquid was present in that part of the burned building, charring of this sort points toward a deliberately set fire.

Of course, the most conclusive evidence of arson possible is the discovery of a mechanism or catalyst used to start a fire. There have even been cases where patient investigators have sifted for hours through heaps of ashes and blackened debris, and finally come up with the damaged but unconsumed remains of a fire-setting device.

Sometimes they come upon all the arson evidence they need by sheer good fortune. One of the most fortuitous catches on record occurred in a development of vacation cottages bordering a lake in New York State, when firemen summoned to fight a fire in one bungalow discovered an incendiary setup about to go off in a neighboring bungalow. A fireman had mounted to the roof of one building in order to aim his hose at the blaze, and from this vantage point he could plainly see through the window of the neighboring cottage an arson device almost ready to go off. Both the burning building and its neighbor that was set up for burning were owned by the same man. He was subsequently convicted of having set fire to his own property to defraud the insurance company.

But such swift discovery of the physical evidence of arson does not take place every day. Usually the investigation of the site of a suspicious fire requires long hours, sometimes several days, before the local officials and the special agent of the National Board are satisfied. Nor is their satisfaction enough. They must obtain evidence, if they can, that may be used in court either to convict the arsonist or, short of this, to defend the insurance carriers against a suit for payment.

In one such suit in Westchester County, New York, successfully defended in 1953, an important piece of evidence consisted of several glass jars filled with dirt. The significant point was that the dirt contained traces of kerosene, the presence of which was certified by a chemical laboratory that tested it. In looking into this fire, a highly suspicious one that destroyed a resort hotel, the arson investigators traced the origin of the fire to the basement stairs, where they noticed a faint odor of kerosene. It emanated from a point at the foot of the basement steps where the concrete paving had broken. The fuel had evidently seeped into the ground and been held there as in a blotter. The probers scooped up a sample of the dirt, sealed it in sterile jars and sent it to the lab for analysis. This discovery, by men who knew what they were hunting for, and where, helped clinch a case involving insurance claims amounting to $140,000.

In the case of a 200-room resort hotel in Florida that was totally destroyed by fire in 1959, the vital evidence of a deliberately set fire came from the condition of the hotel's sprinkler system after fire had burned up almost everything else. Inspecting the sprinklers to find out why they had not operated during the fire, the investigators found that the sprinklers in the center wing of the hotel had been cut off at a control wheel, which had been turned at least fifteen times. The cutoff controlling the east wing sprinklers was operated by a handle, and this was assumed to be in an open position when the inspection seal was in place, as it was following the fire. But a closer look revealed that the top portion of the handle was loose, and further inspection showed that this part had been removed with a wrench and the sprinkler system cut off at this point. The handle had then been replaced, thus making it appear that the sprinkler system was on, whereas it had been cut off. There was no doubt, therefore, that someone wanted to burn down the hotel.

The special agent's work is far from finished when it has been determined that a fire was deliberately set. He must next find out, if possible, who set the fire and why. Sometimes discovery of the "who?" readily answers the question "why?"; sometimes it is the other way round. A clear motive may, in the best detective-story tradition, point to the guilty arsonist. There are enough exceptions to all rules, however, to make this part of the special agent's task most exacting. For even though it can be proved that a fire was deliberately set, the assured has a right to his fire insurance payment unless it can be shown that he was involved in the arson. He may have been the victim of an enemy who sought to do him harm by firing his premises. Or his property may have been the target of a pathological fire setter, who selected his building to burn by sheer chance, and not for any logical motive. If he is to complete his task, therefore, the investigator for the National Board must put all the pieces together accurately in the case of a fire that he knows definitely to be of incendiary origin. Simply proving that a suspicious fire was set and leaving the case there would be to abandon it at the crucial point.

Certain familiar signs can direct the investigator's suspicions to the policyholder. Primary, as one might suspect, is evidence of a failing business, at least in the case of a business property fire. "Selling out to the insurance company" is an old story among failing small businessmen, some of whom when confronted with the evidence of their guilt seem to have no realization of the seriousness of the crime of arson. In their concern to turn a losing business into cash by fire, many think that their offense is mitigated by the fact that the cost of the fire is spread over many thousands of people in insignificant amounts. They give no thought to the possibility that the fire they light can lead to the injury or the death of firemen, or of innocent people who might be caught in neighboring property.

In order to find out just what was the financial condition of the assured before the fire, the special agent and the official investigators of the city interview suppliers, customers, neighbors, credit agencies, banks and any other source that can help fill in the picture. Because most fires arising from business failures are a last, desperate resort of worried and not especially clever men, the signs of a sick business are usually easy to discern. The investigator always interviews the assured, and can sense he is on the right track if he finds that the policyholder tries to bluff about the health of his enterprise. Likewise, if the assured refuses to answer questions in a straightforward manner this fact can lead the investigator to think that he has guilty knowledge of the fire. Not uncommonly a guilty assured will break down under questioning and confess to arson, primarily because he is not a hardened, habitual criminal and he is unused to feeling the heat of an interrogation. In such cases it may turn out that firing his property was a hasty act of a cowardly individual, who is genuinely relieved to expiate his crime, as he thinks, by confession. More frequently, however, the perpetrator of arson to defraud will require more convincing, in the form of a very solid case against him backed up by strong evidence, before he will confess.

It would never do, of course, for the National Board's special agent to consider a case complete because he had established that the victim of a deliberately set fire had profited financially from it. Where it is established that the insurance money is more than the value of a sick business, a possible motive is all that has been found; but this is not proof that the assured was involved in setting the fire. Any business in trouble can suffer an accidental fire. Or it can be burned by an outsider, such as a personal enemy or a business rival of the policyholder. Therefore the investigator must establish the whereabouts of the suspected person just before the fire, in order to prove that he could have set it. The employment of a professional "torch," a criminal whose specialty it is to set off fires for pay, can help the businessman establish a good alibi.

But no criminal can be trusted, and this rule is doubly valid for those who hire themselves out as fire setters. In hiring him the dishonest policyholder risks disclosure, should he fail to pay off the torch in full and on time. When a company holds up payment of a claim on the strength of an Arson Department warning that the fire is suspicious and is under investigation, a hired fire setter whose payment hangs on his client's collecting the insurance may change his colors. If he feels the investigators closing in, he may panic. And if he feels the law closing in on his client, the hired torch will often turn state's evidence against the one who hired him, in the hope of lenient treatment from the prosecutor.

In its first fifty years the National Board of Fire Underwriters fought against arson almost entirely through the use of a reward fund, to which various companies offered contributions for the solution of specific arson fires. The Committee on Incendiarism and Arson, as it was then called, made payments from the fund at its discretion. In this period there was no Arson Department, and therefore no staff carrying on the functions described in the preceding pages. By 1916, when the National Board was a half century old, it had become clear that the reward fund method was not achieving results, since in that one year the member companies offered 160 different rewards totaling $43,000 in the hope of checking a wave of arson—yet only two rewards of $500 each were paid in the year. In fact, the record shows that during the first half-century of the National Board's life nearly $2,200,000 had been offered in rewards, and only $87,324 had been paid.

The foundation of the present-day Arson Department was laid early in 1917 as America prepared to enter World War I. It was, in fact, the result of a general fear among government officials as well as responsible executives in manufacturing industries and the insurance business that agents of the Central Powers might turn to industrial sabotage by arson and bombing. The National Board set up a small Investigation Department, which began work on February 1, 1917, with two investigators—F. R. Morgaridge and Henry J. Sloan, both recruited from the Illinois State Fire Marshal Department. Three more men were added shortly afterward. This department of five, headed by Morgaridge, concentrated its inspection on the

Middle Atlantic and New England states, the most likely danger area for sabotage of war materiel in transit and storage before overseas shipment.

A report by Morgaridge to the National Board, dated September 17, 1917, reveals that as early as that first year of its work the arson-investigating arm of the National Board had already set the pattern of restraint and caution that marks its present approach. Morgaridge wrote at the time:

> We have assisted the Department of Justice at Washington in the investigation of some fires which appeared to have been caused by alien enemies. Mr. A. B. Bielaski has called on us for assistance in a number of cases. Mr. Sloan went to Saginaw, Michigan, on one of these cases, and found that instead of the fire being caused by a German spy it was in reality caused by one of the employees of the factory.

Later in his report the Investigation Department chief, perhaps impatient with the wartime tendency of the hysterical to see an enemy agent behind every tree, commented in regard to fires in big factories and warehouses:

> As a matter of fact, more disastrous fires in such buildings are caused by notoriety-seeking watchmen than from any other class of incendiary.

It is notable, likewise, that from the outset the National Board's policy was to work with local officials at all times, never in conflict with them.

The Mr. Bielaski of the United States Department of Justice mentioned in that first report later joined the National Board staff, and headed the Arson Department for thirty years, from 1929 until his retirement in 1959. During this period the department grew to approximately its present size. Some of its busiest times came during the early years of the great depression, when many small businesses failed and a number of unprincipled owners sought a desperate way out by means of a so-called "business fire." A particularly notorious and unsavory arson ring centered in Brooklyn, New York, was brought to justice at this time, largely through the efforts of Mr. Bielaski and his men, who doggedly hunted down an infamous torch and a firm of crooked insurance adjusters who worked in active partnership with him. In fact, the torch referred his "clients" to the adjusters, and they, in turn, referred "clients" to him.

Another case, which might have been funny had it not been so serious, involved the trapping of a master fabricator of delayed-action incendiary devices, who turned out to be an almost illiterate Chicago grandmother. When interrogated after being caught, she made it clear that she looked on her specialty with great pride as a form of workmanship that approached a fine art. Her devices were complex affairs that included a fuse, a sticky blob of wax and a great cluster of sulphur matches; yet despite the fact that she lavished hours putting together each "fireball" and was sometimes days behind in filling orders, she stubbornly insisted on maintaining her price of only $15 apiece! To her, pride in her "art" was even more important than money.

World War II brought an end to depression conditions. America in 1940 and 1941 was quickly transformed into the Arsenal of Democracy, producing, packaging and shipping a great variety of goods for the war effort. Suddenly business was good almost everywhere. Nothing was surplus; everything was in short supply. The "business fire" disappeared. In close cooperation with security agencies of government the National Board arson investigators shifted their attention and kept on the alert for signs of enemy sabotage by fire and bombing. Yet World War II passed into history with no firm evidence that an agent of the Axis Powers succeeded in any sabotage attempt.

The postwar years have witnessed a rapid increase in public concern over youngsters, their relationships with their families, their attitudes toward schooling, and an apparent breakdown of young people's respect for law and property. As a nation Americans have become conscious of the fact that since World War II deep-rooted changes have taken place in youth attitudes and youth behavior. The Arson, Theft and Fraud Department of the National Board has become acutely aware of these changes from its own special viewpoint, as the record of arson by juveniles and youthful thrill seekers has proven.

Literature from the earliest times testifies that mankind has always been attracted to fires. Boys, especially, thrill to the sound of the fire engines, and are usually among the first to reach the scene of a fire. Their youthful impressions of the mixture of tragedy, awe and heroism that a fire and the fire fighters symbolize together have been lasting ones, carried through life. Yet it has been only in the years since World War II that fire setting by young people has become such a serious part of the incendiarism problem. Sometimes fire setting by juveniles has been found to have been a group action, committed by perfectly sane but undisciplined youngsters whose idea was to create excitement. One such fire, planned and set in 1955 by a group of teen-age girls who belonged to a high-school club in Memphis, Tennessee, completely destroyed a building on the city fairgrounds. Again, in 1954 a vacant farmhouse in Michigan was set afire by a clique of high-school boys and girls just after graduation in June. It came out that the youngsters had been using the empty house for a juvenile lovers' rendezvous, and now that their school days had come to an end and the regular parties in the house were over, they wanted to destroy the house so no other couples could use it. All were from respectable families and none had been in trouble of any kind. These are but two examples among many in the National Board files.

In tracing down the cause for these and similar fires, the Arson Department special agent must rely on his acquired knowledge of juvenile behavior patterns and his layman's appreciation of the psychological factors involved. The same holds true in the case of the pyromaniac, or pathological fire setter. The National Board representative understandably does not get into that part of handling pyromaniacs, once identified, that is the province of the trained mental-health specialist. But he is an old hand at identifying signs of abnormal arsonists at work and calling the attention of the civil authorities to them.

Basic to these signs is repetition—the same kind of property set on fire, the same method used to start a series of fires, or several fires within the same small area. Special agents have found, for example, pyromaniacs who repeatedly set fires with a few papers placed in or under a baby carriage left in the hallway of a tenement house. One "pyro" actually followed a lunar cycle, feeling the impulse to light a fire only with the full moon. In some cases a pathological fire setter will join actively in fighting the fire that he has set, and it has emerged that he seeks his primary thrill in the noise and speed of the fire-fighting apparatus, rather than in contemplating the mounting flames. Many fire setters actually join volunteer fire companies in order to indulge their secret passion, and not uncommonly such unstable firemen are caught early in the game. Certain pyros derive a sexual thrill from being close to the flames and observing the excitement all around them. The world of the pyromaniac, in short, is a strangely distorted, unreal world of entangled fact, fantasy and sensation.

The most direct contribution that the special agents of the National Board make in restricting the damage done by such people lies in helping to apprehend them as soon as possible. Frequently the special agents are called upon to address arson seminars, extension courses in arson investigation and detection offered by universities, and conventions of fire chiefs. At these meetings they have an opportunity to discuss abnormal fire setting. Many fire-chiefs in rural communities have little or no other way of learning about pathological fire setting.

The National Board has made a unique contribution toward public enlightenment on this subject by underwriting a definitive study of pyromania by Drs. Nolan D. C. Lewis and Helen Yarnell of the Department of Psychiatry, Columbia University. The results of the Lewis-Yarnell research were published in 1951 by the Coolidge Foundation.* Until further advances are made in clinical work on this aspect of mental illness, *Pathological Firesetting* remains the one significant source book for mental-health workers.

There are many lines of distinction drawn by the arson investigator between various kinds of arson. These distinctions are primarily motivational, and they become blurred as one moves from the sane, criminal end of the spectrum, where financial gain is the one motive, toward the totally irrational, pathological case on the other. Yet with all the blurring, the distinctions are important in so far as they help the investigators to determine who set a particular fire. The most common sort of fire for profit is

* *Pathological Firesetting (Pyromania)*, by Nolan D. C. Lewis and Helen Yarnell. (New York, Coolidge Foundation, Publishers; 1951)

the fraud fire, where the arsonist is a policyholder who seeks to defraud his insurance company. But there are other kinds of fire for profit, or gain. Building contractors have been known to arrange fires in order to create a demand for their services. There is the case of the watchman, worried lest his job be abolished, who "discovers" a fire in order to emphasize the need for his services. Other employees have set fires in order to display to their superiors their heroic devotion to the company by "saving" the firm from a disastrous fire. And occasionally firemen in small communities have seen to it that there is enough "action" at regular intervals so that their place on the payroll is justified. Some have even managed to be heroes at their own fires, at considerable risk, in order to push themselves forward as candidates for promotion. All these are forms of fire for profit, or gain, without being insurance fraud fires. The National Board is, of course, equally concerned with both kinds of arson.

"Hate" fires border on the pathological, and the determination of whether the hate arsonist should be sent to a penal or to a mental institution is in the province of the courts. Classified under the heading of hate fires are those set in the sudden flush of anger which one person feels toward another. This kind of impulse arson is committed within a very short time, usually within hours, of the offense which impelled it. Not being planned carefully and with stealth, it is often easy to trace to the guilty arsonist. Somewhat more difficult to detect is the so-called "spite" fire, which one person may set in order to do harm to another against whom he may have nursed a grudge for some days or weeks. Lovers' quarrels, husband-wife discord, employer-employee fights and similar elements lie at the origin of spite fires. Like those set in sudden anger, they can frequently be solved by interviewing the owner of the premises in order to find out who may have a grudge against him. The fire for revenge is a somewhat different type of arson, because the motive of the fire setter may be based on some real or imagined injury at the hands of the property owner so long ago that the victim of the fire has long since forgotten it. This kind of hate fire may be extremely difficult to detect, because there may be nothing that the property owner can tell the investigators that will lead them to someone with a motive for setting the fire.

One other kind of hate fire, that based on racial or religious antagonism, was not uncommon in the nineteenth century when the great waves of immigration to America placed groups with their imported Old World hostilities in close and competitive proximity. The first part of the twentieth century found such fires becoming less and less frequent as Americans tended toward harmonious social amalgamation. But there has been an upsurge of this kind of hate fires combined with bombings in the South in the 1960s, especially in Mississippi, directed against Negroes active in the civil-rights movement. The particular problem that arises in these cases, one which the National Board of Fire Underwriters cannot solve alone, is that of indifference on the part of law enforcement agencies in certain places over catching those who are guilty.

There are times when arson is not the primary aim of the fire setter, but rather is a result of another crime. Embezzlers have been known to set fires in order to destroy the documents that would prove they had been stealing. Burglars and pilferers have turned to fire as a means of covering up their thefts. And there have been cases when a murderer sought to conceal his crime, even to destroying the corpse, by setting a house on fire.

An amazing case of combined arson-murder was solved in Connecticut in 1944, close to a year after the double crime was committed. In September 1943 a fire destroyed an empty summer cottage on a Connecticut lake. Circumstances pointed to "tramps or kids," according to the authorities, but no suspect was apprehended. The following May the owner's wife was raking up the debris when her rake caught on something from which it would not come loose. She bent down to free the rake and found it had been caught on a human foot. State police officers were summoned, and they uncovered the charred remains of what appeared to be a woman, with a small hole in the skull apparently made by a bullet. The police eventually identified the body as that of a high school girl who had been missing since the time of the fire, and from her the trail led to a seventeen-year-old boy. Eventually he confessed to having induced the girl to run away from home with him eight months before. He led her to the house at night, raped her, then after spending the night with her he shot her in the back of the head and sought to conceal the murder evidence by setting the house afire with the body in it. So confident was the boy that he had committed "the perfect crime" that he even wrote a boastful theme in high school under that title, giving his teacher the impression that he had a vivid imagination. He would have been caught long before if the ruins of the fired cottage had been carefully examined in the first place.

In its drive to control arson, the National Board of Fire Underwriters for years advocated the enactment of a model arson law in the various states. Such a law treats arson as the serious offense that it is, and provides varying prison sentences for conviction of arson in any one of four degrees. It also defines burning in an attempt to defraud the insurer as a felony carrying a penitentiary sentence of from one to five years. More than forty states have enacted such a model arson law.

A hopeful step taken by an agency of the federal government in cooperation with local law enforcement agencies provides a statistical aid in the war against arson. In response to a request brought by the International Association of Chiefs of Police and strongly supported by the National Board, the Federal Bureau of Investigation starting with the calendar year 1964 began collecting statistics for the entire United States on the number of arrests made in arson cases. No one had the resources or the authority to do this job before, and the FBI up to this time lumped arson arrests together with those for a number of other crimes, so that they could not be distinguished. However, starting with the compilation of its *Uniform Crime Report* for the year 1964 (issued summer 1965) the FBI provides figures by which progress in the arrest of arsonists can be gauged.

A further weapon against arson, which the National Board helped to bring into the fight, is the recent extension of federal authority to act against interstate arson criminals. The Justice Department had long before been given statutory power by Congress under the commerce clause of the federal Constitution to pursue auto thieves, white slavers and other interstate criminals. Adding to its criminal jurisdiction the pursuit of interstate arson is an aid in the endless, expensive and frustrating war.

VI

THIEVES, FRAUDS, AND INLAND MARINE LOSSES

"I'VE BEEN ROBBED!"

Every week throughout the calendar year insurance agents in all parts of the country answer the ring of the telephone to hear the same sad story. A client has been the victim of theft, and wants to collect insurance. More often than not it is a case of burglary in a private residence, from which insured jewelry was taken. Otherwise the loss is likely to have involved furs, merchandise stolen from a warehouse or a retail store, even a shipment of pharmaceutical products hijacked from a truck. In the average week, insured-theft claims in the United States add up to well over $1,000,000—exactly how much no one knows.

For a good many years companies writing fire insurance have also written theft coverage of personal articles of value under so-called all-risk or inland marine forms of policies. In addition, certain types of all-risk policies have traditionally covered cargoes in transit or stocks of merchandise such as jewelry and furs. The prosperity of the post-World War II period brought a marked change as a new and affluent middle class acquired expensive furs and jewelry that it had never owned in the depression years before 1941. It followed logically that with this rapid dispersion of stealable things of value, the companies not only found they were writing much more theft coverage, but were also being asked to pay claims at an unprecedented rate. So the underwriters, through the instrument of the National Board, became increasingly concerned with protecting the public against losses by theft.

Most people who have lost insured valuables earnestly hope that the police will somehow recover their stolen property, which they value beyond the cash that insurance might bring. But the record proves that a few sometimes seem more interested in the insurance payment than in getting back their missing property. There are even some whose property is not really missing, and who are deliberately attempting to defraud the underwriter. Sifting the one from the other—recovering stolen property, detecting fraud and preventing theft—amounts to a task of national scope, in which the interests of the insurance business merge with that of the general public. Both companies and the insured public want to see to it that honest losses are fairly paid but that fraudulent claims are not. Both want to curb losses from theft as much as possible, because every loss of property to a thief, if insured, is first paid for by the companies, and later is reflected in the premiums paid by everyone else. In principle, the sequence is just the same as in losses by fire.

It was against this background that in October 1948 the National Board of Fire Underwriters assigned to its investigative department new duties relating to theft of insured property. The department until that time was known as the Incendiarism and Arson Department; later its title was changed to the Arson, Theft, and Fraud Department, reflecting its wider sphere of activity. While the bulk of its attention, perhaps 85 per cent to 90 per cent, remains in the fight against arson, most of the special agents in the department have been trained to investigate theft claims, in addition to their work on suspicious fires. At the same time, the department includes a few specialists who work on theft exclusively, without touching arson work. Because theft investigation involves quite different techniques and problems, this service of the National Board is considered separately here.

In the language of the insurance business, insurance of movable property, that property "not of a fixed nature," falls under the heading of "inland marine" insurance. This old-fashioned term stems from the time when goods in overland transit to or from a port were insured separately from the marine insurance policy that covered them aboard ship. Modern insurance against many kinds of theft—burglary, robbery, hijacking, and larceny, among others—has grown as an extension of the inland marine policies of yesteryear. This somewhat quaint title still serves as a useful nomenclature umbrella covering them all, and it is in frequent use today among insurance men.

Close to two-thirds of all inland marine investigations conducted by National Board special agents are cases of burglary. Technically, burglary refers to loss suffered through the thief's breaking and entering the premises of the victim by stealth. The typical burglary with which the department deals involves jewelry stolen from a residence. In most cases, this means a private house, but apartment buildings, hotel rooms, and motels are frequently the scene of this form of crime. Disregarding cash, which is not insurable above a modest limit, jewelry is by far the most common prey of the thief, for a combination of reasons: the thief can easily see it displayed, he can conceal it after the theft, he or an accomplice can transform or disguise precious stones by cutting them, and he can dispose of them through a cut-rate buyer of stolen goods—known as a "fence." Precious stones are quickly sold in today's continuous, demanding jewelry market, and metal mountings are easily melted down into salable bars.

After jewelry, furs place second as a target of burglars, for about the same reasons. Furs are not only displayed by their proud owners, but they are also removed from the person and are often left carelessly lying about in a public place. A fur thief can sell stolen loot quickly, because there is a thriving demand for it on the fringes of the underworld.

Crimes other than burglary which agents of the National Board investigate include, in descending order of frequency: larceny (theft without necessarily breaking and entering); robbery, in which physical coercion or force is used to overcome the victim; theft from interstate shipments, which the National Board classifies separately because it is covered by federal statute; hijacking of cargoes from trucks, and sometimes stealing the loaded truck; fraud thefts, accomplished through misrepresentation and fast talk; and cases of "mysterious disappearances"—in which the victim has no idea how the loss occurred, but only that the insured property is missing.

During the past few years, with minor variations, special agents of the department have carried out about six hundred investigations of insured losses each year. In most of them the victims were insured by member companies; but in a few instances where this was not so, the National Board of Fire Underwriters entered the investigation as an aid to the police, on the theory that an uncaught thief remains a menace to the member companies and to all policyholders.

The National Board does not investigate every insured loss, because there are too many for this to be practical. It must concentrate on the most important. It does, however, collect loss data on a tremendous scale as an aid both to the insurance business and to the law enforcement agencies. Since 1948 it has received reports from member companies and from a companion group, the Inland Marine Underwriters Association, in each case involving:

1. Lost or stolen jewelry or furs if the loss is of a suspicious nature, or if the loss exceeds $1000;
2. Loss by theft from trucks if the loss is of a suspicious nature, or if the loss exceeds $1000;
3. Hijacking losses regardless of the amount;
4. Loss by fire on trucks if the loss is suspicious, or if the loss exceeds $2000;
5. Loss of any other kinds of property as a result of theft, burglary, robbery, or holdup if the loss is suspicious or if it exceeds $1000; and
6. Fire or explosion loss of any kind if the loss is of suspicious nature, or if it exceeds $2500.

From the outset in 1948, the National Board department charged with inland marine work has urged that channeling all available theft information into one office would turn it into a clearinghouse of benefit to all companies. The centralized file built up in the National Board headquarters soon proved of great value in providing an immediate check on "repeaters"—policyholders to whom making insurance claims became a habit. No one company could reasonably expect to check its claims against the files kept by all other companies. But a centralized file of loss claims, national in scope, has proved most enlightening. In fact, cross-checking inland marine claims against fire-loss claims (see Loss Information Service in Chapter IV) turned up a number of repeaters, who seemed to operate on the assumption that a long lease on

Easy Street could be maintained by collecting insurance on fires, jewelry losses and anything else that came to hand.

The Arson, Theft and Fraud Department turns up loss repeaters every working day. Its files contain some extraordinary and persistent cases: one assured had nine fires in his record, each covered by a different company, and followed them with a like number of claims based on the disappearance of valuables. In another case two related women between them had thirty-six instances of the disappearance of insured valuables before they were stopped. The files of the department have long ago proved their value as a clearinghouse for information in such cases, and those member companies employing it to full advantage spare themselves many a payment to repeaters in the claim line.

Although the department is notified of all inland marine losses of $1000 value or more, it investigates automatically only those where the loss is in excess of $10,000. In addition, it will make an investigation of claims below this figure where the insured has had two or more similar losses, or where it appears that fraud is being attempted by the assured, or where it appears that a professional thief or group of thieves is operating and is responsible for a number of losses, regardless of size. The department investigates all cases of hijacking—typically the overpowering of a truck driver and forcible stealing of the vehicle, or taking the cargo from it. A big delivery truck of high-quality clothing often carries a cargo worth more than $100,000; a truckload of furs or pharmaceuticals can run considerably higher in value.

News of an inland marine loss reaches the National Board from three sources: from a police agency, from an adjuster, or from the loss executive of an insurance company. Much of the time word of the loss arrives promptly, and the trail has not grown too cold for an agent to make an effective on-the-spot investigation. This usually happens in the four cities where most of the loss activity in the United States occurs: New York, Chicago, Los Angeles and the Miami area during the winter vacation season, and where, because of the heavy incidence of losses, the National Board stations special agents who concentrate on inland marine work. There are six inland marine specialists on duty in the New York office, one each in Chicago and Los Angeles, and a mobile detail of agents take up residence in Miami Beach when the crowds arrive. In other parts of the country inland marine investigations are handled by the nearly one hundred special agents who also take charge of arson work.

As in the department's investigation of suspicious fires, inland marine work is always carried out in cooperation with the law enforcement agencies. In the big cities, where inland marine specialists are stationed permanently, they may even accompany police detectives when these officers inspect the theft site and interview the victim reporting a loss. When the agent is called into the case later, he first asks the police what they have learned, then notifies them that he is going to interview the victim and others who may have knowledge of the loss.

There are times when the special agent is the third or fourth person to question the loss victim, who has already been interviewed by the police, the insurance adjuster and possibly someone else from the company with which his policy is written. The policyholder may be tired of the questioning, and may even resent it, as if he thinks he is considered a fraud suspect. The National Board special agent tries to be as diplomatic as possible, and explains that the loss cannot be paid for until his (the agent's) report is turned in. Sometimes the interview that may at first seem annoyingly superfluous actually leads to a clue that assists the theft specialists from the National Board in identifying the thief. In any event, the policyholder has nothing to lose and everything to gain by helping the special agent to learn every possible fact about his loss.

One of the most important elements that the special agent can turn up in the interview is evidence of the thief's *modus operandi*—his method, or technique, of operating, commonly termed his "*m.o.*" by investigators. The agent may learn, for example, that the victim has hosted a crowded, alcoholic open house within twenty-four hours before the theft. This can point to a thief who specializes in mingling in crowds and stealing while the homeowner is distracted by his social duties. Or he may find that the thief surreptitiously unlocked a window or door during the socializing, and returned later to burglarize the premises while the insured was sleeping off the effects of his party. He may conclude that this theft fits into a pattern with others occurring when the same temporary domestic, or catering service employee, was known to have been on the premises before the theft was discovered.

A knowledge of the specialties of thieves is often as valuable to the inland marine specialist as having a thief's picture. The specialty involves not only his *modus operandi* in gaining possession of his loot, but also the kind of valuables he steals. There are, for instance, smooth, self-confident types who dress well and talk glibly, who can pass unnoticed in the crowd at the racetrack, in a hotel corridor or a social gathering, and who do so in order to observe displays of jewelry or furs worth stealing. Some will steal only in hotels; others concentrate on apartment houses. The pattern is probably set by their previous success, because they see no point in giving up a successful *m.o.* There are strong-arm men who go in for hijacking and armed robbery, there are attractive women who victimize men, there are lock experts, safe experts, and sneak thieves who steal valuable merchandise from lofts, warehouses and unguarded trucks. There are specialists who take jobs as domestics, or hotel service employees—and numerous others.

There are thieves who touch nothing but precious jewelry—the most common target. A sub-specialty is the thief preying exclusively on jewelry salesmen, who can carry merchandise worth close to $100,000 in one sample case. There are specialists in the theft of furs, of pharmaceuticals, men's clothing, dresses, and other lines for which they have arrangement for disposal through a "fence," the purchaser of stolen goods. To a surprising degree the nature of the crime can furnish the National Board experts with leads to the most likely suspects in much the way that a graphic artist almost signs his painting by the way he makes his strokes.

It is no denigration of the police force in any jurisdiction to state that the files of the National Board of Fire Underwriters, gathered on a nationwide basis, back up its special agents with more documentation on professional thieves than the police in any one city can collect. Consequently, when the special agent sends in his report to the New York headquarters, it is read there with these questions in mind:

Whose work does this job look like? Who out of prison now could have done it?

The National Board men do not mean "Who in this city?"—but "Who in the entire country?" Amazingly enough, most of the 3000 professional thieves whose pictures and dossiers are in the National Board files are familiar individuals to the inland marine specialists. It is almost as if they had lived with some of the criminals whom they have been watching.

An especially striking example of the efficacy of maintaining a nationwide theft file and a staff familiar with its contents is the case of Grace Harris Jones. There was a period in the late 1950s when this bold and elusive woman skipped from one swank New York apartment house to another, stealing jewelry in quick grabs, then vanishing from sight. Her technique was to knock on apartment doors, posing as a domestic worker reporting to a job, but who was a bit uncertain as to which apartment she was seeking. She would frequently be invited into an apartment by a rich woman delighted to "find" a competent maid by accident. As a variation, she would sneak into an apartment when the door was not double locked, ready with her confused-hired-maid story as an excuse if someone should walk in. She got away with large amounts of insured jewelry before she suddenly disappeared from the New York crime scene. By this time, having been occasionally caught and booked, she was known to the police and to the Arson, Theft and Fraud Department.

Some time passed. Then the New York headquarters began to receive reports of thefts in Chicago that appeared to duplicate exactly the *m.o.* of Grace Harris Jones. Pictures of the Jones woman were shown to the theft victims in Chicago. Yes, they replied, that's the one who talked her way into working as a maid in their apartment, but only long enough to locate the jewelry box. Then she was gone, and the jewelry with her. Eventually, through combining knowledge of the thief's associates and habits held by the police and the National Board, the authorities caught up with Grace Harris Jones. At the time of her last trial and conviction it was estimated that she had stolen close to $1,000,000 worth of jewelry and other valuables. Her total eventually might have run much higher had not the Chicago police been aided by the nationwide resources of the National Board of Fire Underwriters.

There are occasions, though proportionally very few, when the investigating special agent finds something not quite right about the loss as reported by the assured. His suspicion may be aroused by significant discrepancies between the testimony given to the police in an earlier interview and that given to him later. The alleged burglary of a residence may be devoid of any physical evidence of breaking and entering—nothing to indicate a forced lock, no jimmied window, no footprints in the garden, no witnesses to a prowler or a strange car. There can even be signs that the setup was too good for a burglary—that everyone had vacated the scene of the theft, all the servants, the family members, even the dog.

However suspicious the claim may appear, the inland marine investigator reports the facts, and carefully avoids making any recommendations to the company at risk or the adjuster that the claim not be paid. The report emphasizes what the special agent found, what he was told, and what he looked for and failed to find. Yet the final conclusion as to what course to follow rests solely with the company. The National Board's agent's investigation is only an aid, not a compulsory guide.

Inland marine specialists are well aware of the fact that claims which may at first seem based on preposterous stories frequently turn out to be quite valid. There is an instance, for example, of a robbery claim made by a woman living in a prosperous suburb who said that on Halloween when her husband was away she answered the doorbell, and a group of juvenile hoodlums had pushed their way into her house. She stated that they tied her up with cord cut from her Venetian blinds, then stole several firearms and pieces of jewelry before leaving the house. She asserted that she rolled down a flight of steps and called a neighbor for help to free her from her bonds.

The story did not seem to make sense when it was first related to the police and the insurance investigators, who remained highly skeptical. But shortly after the claim was filed, police in a neighboring town arrested several boys with firearms answering the description of the claimant's property. The juveniles subsequently confessed to the oddly conceived crime exactly as the woman had outlined it. From cases such as this the National Board investigators are prepared for the unusual as well as for true-to-type instances of theft.

Time and time again theft reports reaching the National Board prove the old lesson that many victims of loss practically invite burglary. This point was made at the 1963 meeting of the American Association for the Advancement of Science, held in Cleveland, in an address by Michael Fooner of the Association for Applied Psychoanalysis. Affluent people, Fooner told the meeting, invite larcenies and burglaries through carelessness and carefree display of their money and property. He said that the victims of theft need re-education perhaps more than the criminals if the country's property crime rate is to be curbed. They need to know that cars should be locked, and that articles of value should not be left in view even inside a locked automobile. Past studies have proved, Fooner went on, that a great deal of theft is due to what he called "temptation-opportunity situations," which carry a "here-I-am-come-take-me" message to criminals.

"Prevention," Fooner declared, "is better than apprehension of criminals, and it is cheaper."

The National Board's chief special agent in charge of inland marine investigation spoke in similar vein in 1964, at a meeting of the town council in the Long Island suburb where he resides. The group was discussing ways of meeting the problem of a rising theft rate in the town. Asked by the mayor to put his views in writing for the enlightenment of his neighbors, the National Board staff member drafted an instructional brochure on the prevention of residential burglary that was picked up and circulated by the press in several parts of Metropolitan New York. Among the points stressed in his memorandum:

Lights—a well illuminated house is less susceptible to burglary. Lights in rooms not capable of being checked from outside as to occupancy are a deterrent to burglars. It may be well before retiring to leave a front and rear light on.

Residence should be well secured and all doors locked, including garage doors even if left unoccupied for even a brief time.

Do not attempt to convert your home into Fort Knox. Irrespective of the protection you may apply to your residence, if you keep an excessive amount of valuable jewelry and cash, it will be a target for burglary or robbery. Use a bank safe-deposit box no matter how inconvenient.

Avoid being ostentatious in the use of jewelry and furs at your hairdresser, dress shops, parking facilities, race tracks, night clubs and even country clubs. You soon become a target for either a burglary or a robbery. Professional thieves have sources of information in many fields.

Do not discuss your personal and social activities and movements with strangers, nor should you notify the local newspaper about your forthcoming vacation; many burglars make a careful study of the papers for just such accommodating items.

Be your neighbor's keeper. Report immediately to the police any suspicious-looking person, automobiles, or service trucks. Note license numbers. Pay particular attention to your neighbor's residence if you know it is unoccupied, and report unusual or suspicious activity.

Vacation time, with its trips and long weekends away from home, is a favorite season for housebreakers, and Christmas time is also high on the list. When you leave home, lock windows and doors; don't leave notes explaining your absence and don't leave the key. Eliminate as much as possible any indication that you are absent; stop deliveries of mail, milk, and newspapers. Ask neighbors to remove circulars from your mailbox and keep an eye on house and property.

Call police to check on all strange solicitors not carrying proper credentials. Many thieves pose as salesmen or repairmen so they won't arouse suspicion while they are actually studying the premises. Never allow a solicitor of any type to enter your home without satisfactory credentials.

The same principles stressed in this memorandum on ways to prevent burglary in residences apply as well to theft elsewhere. The assured can greatly reduce the likelihood that his or her property will be stolen if potential thieves are not given a helping hand, whether it is in the store, warehouse, loaded van, hotel room, automobile or place of public assembly. The show-off and braggart who must assert himself by a flamboyant display of affluence is asking for trouble. The person who wears jewelry and furs with taste and handles money discreetly has the best chance of retaining his or her property.

The loss experience in the Miami, Florida, area during the winter vacation season illustrates how serious the theft problem can be in a posh resort. In the early 1950s claims for insured losses in Miami (almost entirely jewelry, and more than 80 per cent insured by National Board companies) approached the half million dollar mark every winter. After 1955 the annual losses rose with startling speed until they reached the amazing figure of $1,166,991 in 1959.

At the outset of the following season the Federal Bureau of Investigation and the Miami newspapers undertook a novel educational project aimed at the entire resort community. On one morning the people of Greater Miami found plastered on the front page of every newspaper the pictures, names, local addresses and criminal records of fifteen notorious thieves then in Miami. These men were known by the authorities to have been active in the area for many years, when they were out of prison. Some of these criminals suddenly felt that Miami had become too hot for comfort, and left the city. This campaign of public enlightenment doubtless had much to do with the resultant drop in insured loss claims from Miami that winter, to a point scarcely more than half that of the previous season. But the effect was not permanent, and the loss rate in the Miami area is again in the million-dollar class, because there are always new show-offs who feel compelled to flaunt their riches, and thieves on the prowl for them. The loss ratio is also on the rise in the newer resort areas of Arizona and Nevada as well, since they have become playgrounds for the newly rich.

Following the general rule that America is always getting more of everything, total inland marine losses are gradually on the rise from year to year. Yet savings and recoveries effected by the National Board's investigative work are also increasing. On a national scale, the department's antitheft and fraud program has proved its value from the beginning in hard cash savings to the member companies. This leaves to one side the other function of inland marine work—its value as a deterrent—which cannot be calculated accurately because no one can say how many more losses would be suffered if the department were not on the job. But the value of stolen goods and articles recovered, combined with the value of doubtful claims either withdrawn by the assured or defeated in court, totaled $830,000 in the accounting year ending in April 1964. This "recoveries and related savings" figure, as it is termed, has risen steadily since the late 1950s. The number of persons arrested in cases investigated by National Board agents has gone up—from 153 in 1960 to 161 and 177 in the two most recent years. The increased success of inland marine investigatory work can fairly be credited to the maturing technique of investigation as well as to the increasingly useful files which the National Board has built in the service of its member companies and the insured public.

For in the end it is the public that benefits from the National Board's seemingly endless war against theft, just as in the long campaign against arson. Yet while the war goes on, the public pays its cost. As total insured losses mount, insurance premiums inevitably follow it upward in a roughly parallel line, area by area. This is why in New York City, where so much wealth is tightly concentrated that it attracts thieves as nowhere else, the rates on theft insurance for jewelry are among the highest in the United States. By enlarging its program to include the investigative work aimed at solving inland marine losses, the National Board of Fire Underwriters has added a new and powerful arm to the forces combating crime against property. By its very nature this work is in the interest of the entire American people, not merely the policyholders. And as in its labors to cut back the waste caused by preventable fires, the National Board urges the public to join the team—by taking greater care in protecting its own property from theft. The chief special agent mentioned earlier put it this way in the memorandum that he prepared for his own fellow townsmen:

> Burglary and robbery are both big business and a profession. But burglars generally cannot do their work alone. They count on your help. It makes much better sense to help yourself and your law enforcement agency instead.

VII

HOW SAFE IS THIS CITY FROM FIRE?

No one can tell if the raging conflagrations that laid waste the heart of San Francisco, Baltimore and Chicago have disappeared from the American scene. But it is certain that the chances of a city's burning up are far less today than they were before San Francisco. This has come about in large measure because the National Board of Fire Underwriters for more than sixty years has been continuously surveying the readiness of the major cities and towns of the United States to fight fire. Almost unknown to the general public, National Board engineers have visited, inspected, and graded the fire defenses of America's principal population centers. Their efforts have helped give rise to a great wave of improvement in building codes, in fire-fighting equipment and in city water supply systems. Today the average city dweller can feel more secure in his place of work, in a store, and in his home at night as a direct result of this continuing fire engineering program. Of what, exactly, does it consist?

Almost every week somewhere in an American city a

fire chief's red car embarks on a mission of special importance to the head of the city fire department. The same car may have raced to a hundred or more fires that year, with siren wailing and red rooftop light flashing. What is special this time is the passenger in the chief's car. He is a visiting fire protection engineer from the National Board of Fire Underwriters.

The department head, whether he is called superintendent, director, or chief, normally goes to fires in order to supervise the performance of his men. He is accustomed to finding the mayor and other city officials on hand occasionally as interested, though not particularly expert, observers. But when he steps from his car with his passenger this time, he knows that the man at his side is evaluating his organization with the eye of a highly qualified specialist in fire engineering. If he ever fervently hopes that every fireman will do his duty effectively, this is the time, for he knows that the National Board engineer knows exactly what to look for.

It is no accident that the visitor accompanied him to this fire. Such an impromptu trip is a regular event in the National Board's continuous process of surveying and grading the fire defenses of several hundred large American cities. These surveys were initiated by the National Board in the wake of the Baltimore conflagration of 1904. They have been developed and expanded through the years to the point where they number about twenty-five to thirty-five complete city inspections annually, and a roughly equal number of supplementary or special inspections. The incidence of fire alarms in sizable communities makes it highly likely that an alarm will sound in department headquarters at least once while a National Board engineer is present. When it does, the department head is usually eager to invite his visitor to ride with him to the fire scene so that he can observe the city fire department in action.

The visitor, a staff member of the Engineering Department of the National Board of Fire Underwriters is one of a three-man survey team. Eight such engineering teams are usually at work throughout the calendar year, three based on the National Board office in New York and the others on the Chicago and San Francisco offices. Nearly half their working time the engineers are on the road surveying cities in all quarters of the United States; the rest of the time they are in the office drawing up the survey reports which are the end product of the fieldwork. From start to finish the complete survey of one city may require anywhere from two or three weeks to several months.

Arrangements for the visit are made by agreement between the city authorities and the National Board. Sometimes the survey is requested by the city. On other occasions the National Board takes the initiative by calling attention to its program of reinspecting every major city at intervals of five to ten years, or as close to it as need and staff time permit. Whoever takes the first step to arrange it, the city authorities are informed of the survey. From the past record of the survey program they know their city will benefit by receiving, free of charge, a frank and impartial evaluation of the municipal fire-defense system, conducted by an outside agency with no political axe to grind. The National Board seeks only to know what the conditions are. On its side, the insurance business gains precise knowledge of the city's chances of preventing its individual outbreaks of fire from spreading into multi-block conflagrations.

Obvious benefits flow as a matter of course from the detailed printed report, augmented by maps and tables, in which the National Board summarizes the findings of each city survey. Conscientious municipal authorities usually take the criticisms embodied in the report to heart, and try to remedy deficiencies in their local fire-prevention and fire-fighting system within the limits of their means. Frequently they learn of shortcomings of which they were not aware, until the National Board survey brought these deficiencies to their attention. Whatever improvement in the city's fire protection that results is of benefit to everyone, the uninsured as well as the property owners carrying insurance. Finally, rating bureaus and insurance commissioners use the gradings derived from the survey reports as a gauge for the adjustment of rates. Thus, the surveys provide a means, as accurate as the developing science of fire-protection engineering allows, for keeping the rates in line with conditions. As explained before, however, the National Board does not establish insurance rates.

When the three-man municipal survey team reaches a city, the opening event in its program is usually a conference with the executive head of city government—the mayor or city manager. At this meeting the visitors explain what they plan to accomplish during their stay in town. They outline the procedures they wish to follow and secure the mayor's full backing to insure that his department heads cooperate by opening their records and demonstrating the work of their departments as the visiting engineers request. Since the mayor has already been informed of the purpose and character of the survey, this opening session is usually a get-acquainted meeting at which the inspection schedule is arranged. In most instances the National Board men are given all the help they need in terms of transportation, office space, telephone service and similar courtesies.

Many National Board survey men hold college degrees

in engineering, usually in the mechanical and civil branches, and some are licensed professional engineers. In addition they have also acquired considerable experience in all phases of the art of fire-protection engineering. They are by no means "book men" who are innocent of the practical side of fire-prevention work. They know construction, mechanics, fire-fighting technique, industrial chemistry, water-supply planning and operation—all of which are necessary in fire engineering. They are, in fact, members of a relatively small fraternity of specialists whose particular skill is their all-around knowledge within those disciplines that bear on the problem of fire safety. It is their combination of these skills that qualifies them for this work. Yet as they survey a city, each of the three team members concentrates on his own particular fields of inquiry. One of the party surveys the construction practices and pattern of the city; a second covers the water system; a third inspects the fire department. And although each man busies himself in his own sector, he confers daily with his two colleagues on the interrelations between them. Thus the final report is more than the sum of three separate inspections; it is a synthesis of information gained by three cooperating specialists.

The National Board engineer who concentrates on the fire department starts his inspection by sitting down in conference with its chief, who is in day-to-day operational command. He spends several hours in obtaining the big picture of departmental administration, its man power, and its place in city government. In this interview, as in all the questions asked by the survey team, the National Board visitor does not ask any trick questions. He is not trying to catch anyone off guard. Before he has finished he will have seen most of what he wants to learn with his own eyes. Questions and answers, therefore, figure less importantly than physical evidence in the survey.

Both in interviews and in his inspections throughout the weeks of the survey, the visitor is guided by a 100-page booklet, issued by the National Board, outlining the topics to be covered and the method of evaluating the city's performance under each heading. The booklet bears the unwieldy title: *Standard Schedule for Grading Cities and Towns of the United States with Reference to Their Fire Defenses and Physical Conditions.* For simplicity, however, those who use the booklet refer to it as the "Standard Grading Schedule." The mayor usually has been provided with a copy of the grading schedule, from which he can learn exactly what the inspecting engineers are looking for, and what standards the National Board considers satisfactory on each point.

The visiting engineer does not use the Standard Grading Schedule in an arbitrary way. As he opens his inquiry, the fire department specialist is first concerned with the effectiveness of the department administration. He inquires into the number of officers and men on the department rolls, their distribution, and the deployment of fire stations throughout the city. No fire department can score high marks simply because the city spends a large amount of money per capita on it annually, or because it has a high complement of firemen and officers related to the area covered, or because it has an impressive array of expensive equipment. The entire purpose of the National Board survey is to evaluate the degree of effective fire protection that the department offers the municipality. It must therefore relate the man power and the department's equipment one to the other, and both of these to the conditions in the city. In evaluating the fire-fighting personnel and the department's equipment, the surveyors always bear in mind the old rule: "Fire engines don't fight the fire."

Of thirty-four points devoted to the fire department in the grading schedule, the first seven relate to personnel, their selection, training, strength, etc. In regard to the department chief's tenure of office, for instance, the National Board approves his being secure in his position, provided he is competent, rather than being subject to political appointment and removal. There is too much at stake for a city fire chief to be a political hack appointed under the outmoded spoils system. The schedule covers such other personnel matters as the distribution of officers, their availability at all times, the promotion system within the fire department, method of selection and appointment of new firemen, physical fitness standards and retirement policies. In summary, the National Board survey tries to answer the question: How good are the men in the department, and how well distributed are men and equipment to protect the city from conflagration danger?

Of particular importance is the positioning of fire stations, in terms of running time required for their engines to reach any part of the city for which they are responsible.

After gaining a broad picture of the fire department as a whole, the engineer from the National Board starts on a personal inspection of the fire stations. In most cases he will go over every engine company in the city, devoting perhaps two hours to each. The chief has doubtless informed all hands that the inspector is in town and may appear any day. But because the visitor chooses the order in which he visits the stations, the captain on duty usually does not know that the National Board representative is on the way until he appears.

First the men are assembled, and the inspector can see whether the number of men on hand corresponds to the company strength of which he was told in the chief's office. If a man is out sick, for example, he finds out what procedure is followed to provide a replacement from off-duty personnel. With an experienced eye he can get an impression of the department discipline and morale from the way the company responds to the muster call. Uniforms, state of personal cleanliness, manner of addressing officers and other such details all play their part. One inspector got a quick insight into departmental discipline in a city where he asked a fireman as he approached the station: "Can you please tell me where the chief is?"

"Oh, Jim is out back, I guess," was the casual reply. The visitor drew his own tentative conclusion, later confirmed by further evidence, about discipline in a department in which a fireman referred to his commanding officer by a nickname. The National Board survey teams do not overemphasize such little things, but they are trained to watch for relevant detail that indicates something more important.

Once in the station, the inspector takes a fire company inspection form from his notebook and starts to fill it out. He notes down the type of fire apparatus operated by the company, its make, year, and registration number. From front to rear, topside and underneath, he inspects the fire engine as he has inspected literally hundreds of others through the years he has been performing this task for the National Board.

To the average taxpayer a fire engine is a formidable and somewhat mysterious mechanism that roars past his house or his halted car exhibiting awesome power, without his questioning how good an engine it really is. But to the National Board engineer making his inspection it is an unromantic utilitarian piece of automotive equipment, designed to perform certain functions in the control of fires, paid for by thousands of people who are totally unaware of how good, or how deficient, it may be for that purpose. In a certain sense, he is acting for all those people in his critical examination of their property.

Down on his tally sheet go more than a hundred details such as these: The apparatus engine: What is the make? Number of cycles? Size of bore? Length of stroke? Horsepower at what number of revolutions per minute? The pump: Make? Type? Capacity in terms of gallons per minute delivered at how many pounds per square inch? Number and size of suction outlets? Radio equipment? Number of lengths of hose of each size? The ladders: Material? Length? Method of raising them?

The National Board engineer checks both the company equipment and the men's knowledge of what their engine carries by asking questions of each man. He looks for tools such as axes, bolt cutters and pinch bars that enable firemen to get to the source of flames. And he inspects salvage equipment to see whether the company is adequately prepared to patch up a house against the elements after a fire is extinguished. In the course of examining the equipment, the National Board representative will query the firemen on the way various pieces should be used.

As the National Board engineers have found, there is almost no limit to the ingenuity of American firemen in devising new and imaginative methods for coping with special fire situations. One organization inspected in 1964 showed the visiting engineer a weight-and-chain device used to dislodge burning trash in vertical incinerator shafts (commonly experienced in apartment houses). Another novelty consisted of several plastic bags of bicarbonate of soda, which the department had found effective in smothering fire in a locked mailbox without damaging the unburned mail. Such fires are at times the work of vandals, but more often result when a careless, tired secretary juggling her handbag, mail, lighted cigarette and perhaps other items drops the cigarette into the slot by accident as she mails her letters.

The visitor does not stop at the engine; he inspects everything about the fire station. He tours the firemen's living quarters and marks down any negative features that would impair the men's morale and efficiency. He looks into the company captain's and station chief's records, to insure that they have access to every pertinent fact within their field of responsibility. Such records would include fuel consumption of the engines, test readings on the engine batteries, maps of hydrants in the district, up-to-date street maps, personnel records, training schedules, and logs on each fifty-foot section of fire hose assigned to the station. Since the National Board considers ten years the maximum period during which hose can be considered reliable, each section must be identified, and its record of use and tests should be on file. (The National Board standard calls for annual testing of all hose at 250 pounds per square inch.)

During the course of his survey of the fire department the visitor touches numerous bases other than the chief's office and the fire stations. He inspects the fire-alarm headquarters to see that it is equipped with a system that transmits alarms promptly and without fail to the stations concerned. He checks for equipment to handle the situation in the event of a power failure, or simultaneous fires, or human failure, or the accidental cutting of an alarm cable during road repairs or building construction. In brief, he looks for dependability. In the course of his inspection he will check the performance of selected alarm boxes and note their accessibility and visibility in an emergency to untrained members of the general public. And he will look into the inspection records of the department to determine whether the alarm boxes are tested every sixty days and after severe electrical storms, as the Standard Grading Schedule provides.

The inspector also visits the local telephone exchange, where he finds out what training operators receive in handling frantic calls for the fire engines. Telephone company operators form a valuable addition to the fire department alarm system, particularly in cases where householders telephone for help rather than run to the nearest alarm box. But the operator who does not know the right procedure for relaying the cry for help to the fire department is of no value when she is needed. In many cities new operators are taught to dial the fire department at once and to let the householder speak directly to the fire alarm headquarters. But in certain places the task is far more difficult, because one telephone company may cover an area serviced by several fire departments, each with its own jurisdiction, of which the public is not aware. In places like this, the telephone company employee plays a vital role in getting the call for help to the proper fire department without loss of time. The inspector wants to find out how well she is prepared to do so.

The most spectacular part of the fire department inspector's job is his test of the pumping engines—all the pumpers in service if he can possibly arrange it. For the pumper tests, which may last two to four days in a city of good size, the National Board engineer shows up in work clothes, knowing he is likely to get several good splashings on a windy day, or that leaky hose couplings may spray him with a film of water when the pressure rises to test level. For the department chiefs, the pumper tests are the moment of truth, because they focus on that part of the department's equipment which represents the greatest expenditure, and on which its success depends. If the pumpers cannot deliver water as required, everything else is crippled.

The pumper is tested by taking water at draft from a river, pond or reservoir. The inspector wants to observe its performance without the advantage of drawing from a hydrant that would deliver water under pressure at the outset. Hose lines are run from the engine, a nozzle is secured in place and fitted successively with tips of various sizes, and the inspector directs the pump operator to start pumping water. When the engine is running and a stream of water is being thrown from the nozzle, the inspector puts his gauge on the stream to check the flow of water.

It is not enough for a pumper to touch the required pressure for a short interval. The inspector directs the operator to turn up his power until it is delivering water through a 1½-inch tip at sixty pounds per square inch, which means 517 gallons a minute, and to hold this level of performance for twenty minutes. By the time the test sequence is completed, the inspector has a pretty good idea of the mechanical condition of the pumping engine and the ability of its operator, whose performance he has been quietly observing. When a large engine is moved away to make room for the next one, it will have sucked up and poured forth more than one hundred tons of water.

While the fire department specialist is going his way, the other two members of the National Board team have spent the first few days of their stay in the city at the drawing table. The engineer specializing in structural conditions, the municipal building department and the city's fire-prevention program has been preparing a structural map of the city. Meanwhile, the water-supply specialist has been working on a map of the water distribution system, which he correlates with the structural map when it is ready for him. His purpose in doing so is to relate the routes by which water is supplied in all parts of the city to the possible needs, in case of fires of various degrees of seriousness.

The structural engineer is sometimes fortunate enough to find that the city building department already has most of what he requires. Often, however, he must piece together his over-all structural map of the city from Sanborn Map Company sheets. There are times when he is forced to go out and "ride the range," as National Board men put it—literally traveling up and down one block after another with a city employee in order to see what kind of buildings there are, and then mark them on his master map, coded according to structure and use.

What gradually takes shape from his work is a large picture of the city showing by colored crayon markings the nature of the construction in each block and the consequent degrees of fire risk. Outlined in green is the principal business district (called PBD by the National Board engineers), in which is concentrated the danger of heavy losses from a spreading fire. In this district special care is taken with inspections. Within its bounds requirements for water are greater than elsewhere, and the area covered by each fire company should be smaller. Both within the PBD and elsewhere on the city map the color code differentiates commercial buildings, manufacturing and hazardous occupancies, public buildings, apartments, and private residences.

After preparing his map, the construction expert walks through the principal business district block by block taking with him large scale maps of handy size on which each building within the PBD is clearly shown. As he makes his tour of inspection, he marks on these sheets the relevant data that could not be learned in the city building department office. To start, he examines the roof line of a building from the street to determine whether or not two adjoining buildings are protected by a parapet. This is a wall jutting upward from a common wall between adjacent structures that protects a roof from being involved by the so-called "mushrooming" effect of a fire in the neighboring building. If there is no parapet above the roof line, a fire that reaches one roof can spread easily to the adjoining roof.

Another safeguard against the spread of fire for which the inspector watches is a wall of sufficient thickness between adjoining buildings, the requirement varying according to the structural load and materials used. In the case of two neighboring buildings with less than thirty feet of space between them, the National Board inspector looks for fire protection of windows by either wired glass or steel shutters. Any of these points that do not meet the National Board standard are marked down as construction deficiencies, in the same way deficiencies are charged to the fire department.

After this external inspection, the National Board representative starts his examination from the inside. As his judgment dictates, he will inspect various buildings in the PBD, and in the course of a week or more he will visit the upper floors of many structures, spending the most time and concentrating his attention on the high value risks. Upon approaching the manager of the business property and identifying himself as an inspector from the National Board of Fire Underwriters he almost invariably gets permission to go to the top floor of the building and work his way down as he pleases. Frequently the owner or manager will have been alerted to his visit by an article in the newspapers or a local business bulletin.

In the principal business district the inspector pays particular attention to floor openings from stairways and elevator shafts. According to the National Building Code recommended by the National Board, all stairways and elevator shafts should be closed off by doors from the corridors on each floor, in order to prevent their being an avenue to spread fire from one floor to another. A closed door prevents a draft of hot air from carrying flames and suffocating gases into the closed-off portion of a building. Fire engineers still bear in mind a tragic memory of the fatal part played by open stairways in 1946 in speeding the spread of fire through the Winecoff Hotel in Atlanta, where 119 people lost their lives. That disaster was just one example in a long list of serious building fires in which open stairways proved a deadly factor.

The National Board construction expert looks for fire-fighting equipment, such as extinguishers, hose and standpipes. He examines inspection tags on the equipment to find out when the city inspectors last paid a visit to this property. He also evaluates the general condition of the building, see if there is rubbish in the stairways that constitutes a fire hazard, find out whether all exits are unencumbered or whether they are blocked inside with merchandise and discarded packing cases and on the exterior by parked automobiles.

In looking over the buildings in this detail the visitor from the National Board gets a picture not only of the way the occupant maintains his property from a fire-safety viewpoint, but also how effectively the city enforces its own fire-safety rules. No other agency, public or private, even begins to undertake such a thorough job of checking on the performance of the officers of local government. The construction man on the National Board team stands in the same sort of relationship to the municipal building and fire-safety officials as the inspector of fire departments does to the fire chief and his deputies. Formally, he represents an association of stock insurance companies; in a broad sense, however, he represents the public interest.

After covering the principal business district, the construction inspector shifts his attention to the rest of the city. While he was piecing together his colored map he compiled a list of representative hazardous properties in various categories which he is especially interested in visiting, because history has proved them to be the most important as fire sources. Most of them are places where highly flammable materials are stored and used. In a motion-picture theater the National Board representative will inspect the projection booth with great care, as well as the stage and the exits. Theater exits are perhaps the one safety feature on which public vigilance is sufficient to keep owners and city officials on their toes, because the lesson of the Iroquois Theatre holocaust of 1903 has never been forgotten. But this does not always hold true of the projection booth of a movie theater, or the backstage area of a legitimate playhouse, where the public does not penetrate.

On this tour the engineer is accompanied by an inspector from the city fire marshal's office, whom he can question both on the fire-prevention code in force in the city (if, indeed, there is one) and the degree to which it is enforced. He can observe, of course, as he poses his questions, and sometimes he comes away with an impression of startling discrepancy between the rules as they appear in print and as they are enforced. By the time he has inspected two or three of each kind of industrial and commercial occupancy, the National Board man is ready to draw some fair conclusions on how well the regulations are observed. As with his opposite number inspecting the fire department, he sets his own schedule of places to visit. It would therefore be impossible for him to be deceived by a little hasty and temporary cleanup or by an elaborate Potemkin village façade. No factory owner can manage, for instance, to install in a rush the kind of automatic fire doors that shut under fire heat (some of them at only 160 degrees Fahrenheit) with the melting of a fusible link that permits a weight to pull the fire door closed.

Aside from inspecting the old buildings that are presently occupied, the visitor studies the new construction under way in the city. He visits building sites with the city inspectors of construction, gas, and electricity in order to determine how well the codes are being followed. This is of particular concern to the underwriters because of the steady rise in building costs. If there is anything deficient in the way they are being built from a fire-safety viewpoint, the underwriters want to know about it. From this inspection of new construction the visiting engineer makes an evaluation of the so-called "trend of construction" in the city, which forms a separate item in his final report. Those concerned want to know the kind of material and style being adopted in the city as a key to its future development—be it glass fronts, ordinary masonry façades, or whatever else the prevailing style may be. And always in dealing with the city departments the inspector is concerned with personnel questions—method of appointment and promotion, size of staff, their qualifications and training.

One part of the inspection that may require a side trip is the determination of how much the city is subject to hazard from aircraft. To accomplish this, the construction engineer confers with the director of the nearby airport (sometimes more than one) to find out the flight patterns and traffic figures bearing on the town being surveyed, and particularly its principal business district.

The task of the water-supply inspector is just as important and as detailed as that of his partners covering the fire department and construction. This member of the National Board of Fire Underwriters team deals with a municipal agency responsible for supplying water to the city. Water with which to put out fires is a side-line product in its total day-to-day operation, amounting to a minor percentage of the city's annual needs. But in case a big fire breaks out, the supply must be sufficient to the fire department's needs all at once. It is the inspector's purpose to find out how well the department is prepared to deliver that side-line product when it is vitally needed.

The visiting water expert's first job is to study the city water-supply map as related to the kind of structures, and consequent fire hazards, on each section of the water system. An amazing intricate thing, the city water-supply map is marked with every hydrant and valve and with every water main leading from the supply points to them. Section by section, the National Board representative studies the map to see whether every section of the city would get water under adequate pressure in the event that simultaneous fires had to be fought close to one another.

An important item in the water department is the maintenance of accurate records. There should be cards on file detailing each valve, hydrant and pipe, located precisely so that repairmen can find out where it is safe to dig. Yet there are cases of National Board surveys turning up utter chaos in the water department records, of which the authorities were apparently unaware because they had left the department to run itself. In one instance the National

Board engineer found that no one knew much about the records since the former water-supply director retired, because, his underlings asserted, "he carried the whole system in his head." The inspector sought out the retired official in his retreat in the mountains to ask him to decipher such water department plans as remained in his old office.

The water-supply specialist visits the city reservoirs, pumping stations and conduits, and takes notes on all features of their administration and operation. Most of his time in the outdoors is spent running fire flow tests of hydrants, which he selects from his water-supply map so as to check the system's performance in several strategic parts of town. He uses a gauge to determine the hydrant pressure and from it calculates the number of gallons delivered per minute. By the time he has finished he has gauged the flow of water from a few dozen hydrants in a small city up to several hundred in a major metropolis.

While the tests measure the flow of water, they also permit a spot check of the condition of the city hydrants, during which it can be seen whether they can be easily opened and put into operation. On occasion the inspection will turn up a defective hydrant, which might have been damaged by an automobile and was not repaired until the National Board inspector came along. Many hydrants today are designed so that the water pressure in the underground pipe holds the valve closed until the handle is turned to open it. This being the case, cities are sometimes slow to discover and repair a damaged hydrant. It is therefore essential that hydrants undergo regular inspection several times a year.

The same situation obtains for water-main valves, which control the flow of water through all parts of the urban water grid. Because it sometimes is important to cut off the water in one section of the system in order to repair a main, all main valves should be in operating condition. Yet the National Board has found that some cities have no program whatsoever for inspecting and testing water-main valves. In fact, it is sometimes discovered during a city survey that a valve has been closed for years without anyone's knowing the difference. The people living in the houses served by the interrupted pipe may never have realized what water pressure they were missing.

When the team has finished its tour of inspection in a given city, their notes are complete, but the calculations leading to the grading of the city will require long days, perhaps weeks, of work back at the National Board office. In the course of their visit the men have reached certain general conclusions, which they share with the mayor in a so-called "exit interview." Speaking in broad terms, yet illustrating their points by specific examples, they give him the highlights of what they have found during their several weeks in the city. In many cases he proves quite eager to learn from the specialists who have been evaluating the city's fire defenses, and displays a conscientious concern over correcting every possible deficiency.

Once they have returned from the field to the National Board office, the members of the survey team set about reducing their hundreds of pages of filled-out forms and notes into a comprehensive report. This is a process of analyzing what has been found in the city just surveyed, and it frequently takes longer than the gathering process. Eventually, long lists of purely factual indications are distilled into numerical grades covering each part of the municipal survey. Each of the engineers does this by totaling whatever deviations from the Standard Grading Schedule have been observed; and by applying the degree of deviation to a table of values he assigns a number of deficiency points under each heading. In this way, item by item, he arrives at a number of deficiency points to be deducted from an ideal, or perfect, score.

The end result of the municipal survey places the city in one of ten classes. It also includes a report, written in paragraph form, describing the visitors' findings in every part of the survey.

The assignment of a final grade to each surveyed city is made only after careful consideration by the supervising engineers of the National Board. The grading is not made public by the National Board; it is submitted confidentially, with printed copies of the survey report, to the executive head of the municipality, who is left to his own discretion as to the use to which he puts it. The grading is also supplied to the state insurance department and to the rating bureau having jurisdiction in the area.

Conscientious city officials are often anxious to eliminate as many deficiency points as possible, to the end that their city will be graded in a higher class as far as fire safety is concerned. If they succeed, their administration can point with pride to the improvement. Even in the course of the National Board team's visit, or when it is imminent, city officials sometimes take steps to improve conditions where they can do so quickly, in order to prevent the city's being taxed with deficiency points that can be avoided. In other cases, when a city has been graded, and falls short of achieving a higher fire-safety rating by only a few points, the city leaders will bring about a number of improvements, which will usually increase the citizens' fire protection, and then ask the National Board to resurvey the city so that it can step up one notch in the grading. Each year several partial surveys are conducted in this kind of situation.

The mere fact, therefore, that the National Board carries out its municipal survey program acts as a spur to improvement, in all parts of the United States, of the capacity of our cities to prevent destruction by fire.

VIII

TESTING FOR PUBLIC SAFETY

TEN! NINE! EIGHT! SEVEN!

The big man in the khaki coveralls and yellow safety helmet boomed the warning countdown through the vast, high-ceilinged workroom. A dozen engineers and technicians moved swiftly to their assigned places and turned expectantly toward the tall furnace. Over the muffled roar coming from the flaming gas ports within, the toll of seconds sounded on.

"Three! Two! One!"

A brief moment of silence, then the bright yellow glare from the furnace portholes quickly faded to black. As the narrow end of the giant heater slid open, a wave of heat struck the nearest spectators. A cloud of dark smoke billowed upward, filling the room. A large wall panel, built into a framework of brick masonry that held it vertical, was pulled out from the furnace by an overhead crane. Glowing red on much of its surface, in other places blackened and cracking, the smoking panel was struck by a hard stream of water from a fire hose. For a few seconds it wavered. Then it yielded to the water pressure, and pieces of the broken panel tumbled to the floor in a mixed cloud of smoke and vapor. The metal studs to which they had been attached stood exposed, twisted and discolored. A photographer's flash stabbed through the murk to record on film the end of the wall panel. Nearby, a cluster of engineers and technicians quietly took down penciled notes on their clip boards.

For the manufacturer of the sample, this had been the moment of truth—the climax of a fire test conducted by Underwriters' Laboratories, Incorporated. Its immediate purpose was to find out whether or not the product he submitted should be listed as safe within the limits of the use for which it was intended. But the long-range purpose of this test, like hundreds of others that are run every working day by the Laboratories, went far beyond that of the manufacturer. It was to help safeguard our entire society from all kinds of hazards—from those that are known and from those obscured in the intricate maze of modern technology.

There was a time not long ago when the term "newfangled" connoted intricacy and a hint of mistrust. But today no one fears the new product. We buy it and use it in confidence that it is safe. Thanks to the testing program of the Underwriters' Laboratories, Americans now live more securely in their homes, confident that they are not in danger from the electricity, gas and oil that serve them. Our people count on the safety built into the lighting and heating systems in places of work and recreation, in common carriers, and in the schools where children spend much of the day. In sum, the Laboratories' program of testing for public safety over the past seventy-odd years has markedly affected the design of a host of materials, products, and devices surrounding us at all hours everywhere.

This is true of the roof overhead and the walls around us. In certain public buildings, for instance, codes require walls that will resist fire for a certain period. The fact that the piece of paneling undergoing the furnace test failed to hold up after being exposed to a heat of 2000 degrees Fahrenheit for three full hours, and then struck by a hard stream of water from the fire hose, did not of itself prove that the product was faulty. It might have been perfectly good as a fire-resistant wall material scheduled to last only one hour in the test furnace, the standard heat test for fire-resistant materials used in single-family homes. In this case, however, the manufacturer had submitted his product to the laboratories for the three-hour test. Had it held firm, the paneling would have met the standard required by many cities for use in multi-story buildings. From its failure the maker learned that he must redesign his product in order to gain the Underwriters' Laboratories' listing in the class he desired. That is why he had paid his testing fee to the Laboratories and submitted his sample section for its ordeal by fire and water.

Underwriters' Laboratories, Inc., has no exact counterpart elsewhere on the globe. It is a nonprofit service organization, not connected with any government agency, devoted entirely to scientific testing of products and materials for public safety. Its costs are paid directly in test service fees by manufacturers selling in the American market. Its purpose is to promote a safer environment for everyone living in our highly technical and increasingly urbanized society. Every living person is, quite literally, a beneficiary of its services. Yet in the more than seventy years during which it has grown from the one-room electrical testing shop set up by William Henry Merrill over the stables of a fire salvage company in Chicago, the public has acquired only the most vague notion of the function of Underwriters' Laboratories.

The original purpose of Merrill's little laboratory was to test the electrical installations at the Chicago Columbian Exposition of 1893. Merrill was employed at first by two groups of Chicago and Midwestern underwriters. Their goal was to curb the danger of electrical fires at the Chicago exposition, which was the first big place of public assembly to be lighted by electricity. Merrill's testing soon after the Chicago fair spread beyond electrical installations to other products, materials and devices that often caused fires. Within a few years the Underwriters' Laboratories, founded with the assistance of the National Board of Fire Underwriters on the base of Merrill's work at the exposition, moved into a wider range of testing against insured perils other than fire. These included disabling accidents, theft and, in recent years, windstorm. Whereas it was the underwriters who at first promoted laboratory testing in order to lessen fire dangers, the clientele that now comes to the UL door consists largely of manufacturers. Today industrial producers actively seek the accolade of its approval. They take pride in their products' being listed by the Laboratories as meeting appropriate requirements and authorized to bear the label: "Underwriters' Laboratories—LISTED."

After more than seven decades the Laboratories are still sponsored by the National Board of Fire Underwriters, and maintain a close working relationship with the insurance business by including a representative group of insurance men on the Board of Trustees. But ever since 1917 UL has been supported entirely by the fees that manufacturers pay for its testing services, with no subsidy from the underwriters. It is a nonprofit service corporation without capital stock. Every dollar of its income is devoted to servicing its clients and, through them, the public. The wording of its certificate of incorporation, under the laws of the state of Delaware, defines its purposes as:

> ... by scientific investigation, study, experiments, and tests, to determine the relation of various materials, devices, constructions and methods to life, fire and casualty hazards and specifications for materials, devices, construction and methods affecting such hazards, and other information tending to reduce and prevent loss of life and property from fire, crime and casualty ...

The principal office and testing station are still in Chicago, the city where Underwriters' Laboratories began, in a long brick structure filling the 200 block of East Ohio Street. Actually, the Chicago headquarters comprise a series of connected buildings, since they have been expanded through the years as the work load on the organization required. Built of fire-resistive construction throughout, the Chicago headquarters house the large vertical furnace used in wall panel tests, chemical laboratories, and rooms for much of the electrical testing, covering about 120,000 square feet of floor space all told.

A second testing station at Northbrook, Illinois, a suburb of Chicago, lies on a spacious property nearly a quarter of a square mile in size. A new building, opened in 1965, has made the Northbrook station the largest of the laboratories. Within a few years the entire Chicago plant is due to be transferred here, because of increasing pressures and costs of operating in the city. At present the fire extinguisher division of the Fire Protection Department of the Laboratories is in Northbrook, as well as departments relating to burglary protection, casualty and automotive testing, and gases and oils testing. Other stations are at

Melville, Long Island, an hour's ride from New York City, where most of the testing is of electrical equipment manufactured in the East; and at Santa Clara, California, not far from San Francisco, where the station provides facilities convenient to West Coast manufacturers for testing most electrical, gas and oil equipment, and certain building materials.

The vertical panel test in the furnace room of the Chicago plant is certainly more spectacular than most of the work at Underwriters' Laboratories, because it simulates the extreme heat conditions of an office-building fire. But simultaneously in other parts of the Laboratories college-trained engineers and experienced technicians are putting all kinds of products through ordeals just as rigorous if less showy—and of just as great concern to the makers. In an electrical testing room, for example, almost any day the visitor can find a number of electric clothes irons which are left operating for 500 hours—nearly twenty-one days—and carefully checked to see whether they overheat, or whether their thermostats continue to function properly. At intervals a tester will drop the irons to the floor, once on each side, on the heel, toe, and sole plate, to simulate the roughest kind of treatment an iron might receive from a careless housewife.

Not far away a half-dozen sections of insulated electric cord are being mechanically, and quite mercilessly, twisted and untwisted, three full revolutions, then back again, hour after hour. Each sample cord is scheduled to undergo 3000 such twistings without cracking the casing or exposing any of the copper conducting wires inside. If any such defect appears, the manufacturer must correct the deficiency and pass the twist test before the cord can gain the UL listing and label. The mechanical contraption that twists the cord is nicknamed a "Rube Goldberg" by

Laboratories men. There are numerous others, so named after the ingenious syndicated cartoonist whose elaborate rigs to perform simple mechanical operations have passed into American folklore and idiom.

Just about every electrical device used in the home or place of work ends up in the Underwriters' Laboratories to be tested for safety against both fire and shock danger. Electric frying pans and coffee percolators are left operating continuously for ten days, primarily to insure that they will not set fire to a wooden surface, such as a dining table, on which they might accidentally be left with the current on. An electric organ, which the home musician might not think harbors the slightest danger, is dissected to see that its internal construction is adequate.

In a mock-up wooden paneling to simulate the tiniest of efficiency kitchens for apartment or trailer, an electric stove is left on at its highest heat for many hours to determine whether it could possibly set the closest wood parts aglow or even char them deeply. If so, UL rejects the sample as unsafe. Even such small devices as light switches are put in the mechanical hands of a Rube Goldberg which clicks them on and off 6000 times, each switching counted on a clock that resembles an automobile mileage instrument.

Television sets are put through most rigorous safety testing at Underwriters' Laboratories, both because they contain such great potential danger and because they are handled by everyone, including young children, in virtually every home in America. Few laymen are aware of the potential implosive force exerted on the TV picture tube, in which pressure is much lower than the fifteen pounds per square inch of the air outside. Should a picture tube suddenly break, the tremendous force of the outside air pressure would drive the heavy glass of which it is made inward (an implosion, as opposed to an explosion), with the danger that sharp glass fragments weighing up to a half pound can be blasted in all directions. Therefore, the screen and the case of the TV set must be so tough as to withstand an accidental implosion of the picture tube if the Laboratories are to list the set as safe. To check a television set for safety, after examining it for fire and shock hazards, engineers at the Laboratories swing a steel ball weighing more than a pound against the outside surface of the viewing screen, to simulate a housewife's bumping it with the end of her carpet sweeper, or a boy's striking it with a baseball bat. If the screen survives the blow from in front, an engineer then tests screen and cabinet from within by driving a steel rod through the cabinet top, so as to cause the picture tube to implode. To pass the test, the screen and cabinet must adequately contain the flying glass from the smashed picture tube. As might be expected, there were some close misses in the television testing end of the Underwriters' Laboratories, when sets produced early in the TV era did not measure up to the standard for listing.

In the so-called "hot rooms" at Northbrook, cooling appliances such as ice makers, refrigerators and window air conditioning units are put through special tortures. The Laboratories men know that a certain number of people will turn off the refrigerator when going away on a summer vacation, hoping thereby to save a few cents' worth of electricity. They overlook or disregard the manufacturers' warning that starting it up again in hot weather imposes an unusual strain on the refrigerator motor. To check whether the motors can take this abuse, new model refrigerators are put in the hot room at 105 degrees Fahrenheit to simulate summer conditions in a top-floor apartment, and are forced through repeated start-up ordeals.

Window air conditioners are not only given a similar hot room treatment, but are also subjected to other indignities. A shower is turned on the exterior part, the water sluicing down at the rate of twelve inches per hour (thus simulating the most intense kind of tropical downpour) to check against water leakage and electrical shock. In addition, a 400-pound weight is placed on the outside section, to test the unit's strength to withstand the weight of the heaviest imaginable window washer.

In every case, testing engineers assume the most careless misuse of equipment by the lazy and ignorant. But they know, too, that in an age of new inventions and gadgets even the educated will not foresee dangers that the manufacturer has overlooked. And they are constantly learning of new ways in which tested material can be mishandled, causing hazards not thought of before. One day shortly after World War II the Laboratories received a startling telephone query from a hotel in Chicago:

"Have you ever heard of a fire started by an electric blanket?" No, the Underwriters' Laboratories spokesman replied.

"We've just had one!" said the caller from the hotel.

Investigation showed that a guest had bunched up his electric blanket into a ball and left it on the hotel room bed with the current still turned on. At that time manufacturers placed electric-blanket thermostats along the edges, but not in the center of the blanket. In this case the thermostats on the outside of the bundle, being exposed to the air, did not react to the intense heat that quickly built up in the center of the blanket, and eventually set both the bed and the room afire. From this experience Underwriters' Laboratories learned that blanket thermostats should be spaced out in all parts of the blanket, and UL distributed this information to the industry.

This chain of events—the relaying of field experience with a specific fire cause to the Laboratories, and its subsequent dispersal by the Laboratories to all manufacturers—has become typical. In this way Underwriters' Laboratories has virtually wiped out dangers that were prevalent not long ago. In the early decades of the automotive era, for example, the Laboratories frequently tested automobile mufflers, service station pumps, and gasoline hoses against the danger of explosion. Today the lessons of that testing have been so completely absorbed by manufacturers that further testing is rarely needed. Electric blankets and TV sets, which required considerable testing and retesting in the late 1940s, are much more often up to listing standards when submitted today. This is also true of pressure cookers, which were involved in scalding accidents twenty years ago but rarely are now.

The loss experience of insurance companies acts as a constant check on the Laboratories' findings, because any unusual loss patterns are quickly fed back to the Chicago headquarters for study. Merwin Brandon, former president of Underwriters' Laboratories, has cited in the following way an episode illustrating the benefits of this liaison between UL and the insurance business:

In the 1930s, when refrigerators were making their appearance in quantities in American homes, markets, and ice cream parlors, heavy fire losses were reported by insurance companies. Staff engineers were immediately assigned to ascertain the cause and obtain correction. Visits to the scenes of some of the fires were made for analysis of the origin of the fires. Few visits were needed to indicate that one of the primary causes was tampering with the factory-installed over-current protection, required by the Laboratories.

Further investigation disclosed that the manufacturers were giving a service contract for one year, and the service men were being called out because of the operation of the fuses provided as a part of the refrigerators. To avoid repetitive calls, these service men replaced the existing fuses with larger sizes. Although this avoided extra calls, the circuit protection to the refrigeration motors was nullified, and fires in the motors or other parts of the machines were transmitted to the buildings.

Conferences with the manufacturers of listed refrigerators produced requirements for either tamper-resistant time-lag fuses, which would operate only when serious overloading resulted; trip-free, manually resettable protection; or inherent over-current protection.

This removed the temptation of the service people to eliminate future calls by overfusing, and accomplished prompt correction of a bad situation. In one month, in New York City in 1930, there were 300 runs of the Fire Department on one make of refrigerating machine. Today, with millions of refrigerators and air-conditioning units in operation, calls on the Fire Department and losses from such equipment are relatively slight.

Summing up the influence of Underwriters' Laboratories in bringing safety directly into the process of manufacturing, UL President Baron Whitaker has said: "We have helped whole industries to bootstrap themselves to higher levels of safety."

Electrical testing accounts for just over one-half of all tests made annually at Underwriters' Laboratories stations, because new electrical devices seem to pour in an endless stream from inventor's mind to drawing board to the assembly line, and thence into the market place. In the 1960s the proliferation of electrically operated vending machines has been at such a pace that the receiving rooms at the Laboratories where incoming samples are unloaded resemble a giant arcade filled with bright, multicolored vendors of every description. Manufacturers are turning out new models every week, selling everything from greeting cards and paperback books to hot and cold drinks and food—and even issuing change in the process. What the average person may overlook is that if a vending machine not made for outdoors use has got wet from rain or leakage, and if he is standing with wet feet in a film of water while putting a coin in the slot, he can—if the circumstances are just right—receive a severe electric shock. Moving an indoors cold drink machine outdoors to the edge of a club swimming pool, for instance, might set up the conditions for this kind of accident. There have been isolated cases of death from such shocks; Underwriters' Laboratories is determined to reduce the possibility of such occurrences. In this the UL has the full cooperation of every manufacturer who submits his vending machines for testing, because he earnestly wants the benefit of UL listing and its label on his products.

In testing fire protection equipment, the Laboratories still check on the performance of so-called "panic hardware," the kind of pushaway bar and latch arrangement that became standard on school and theater doors in the wake of the tragic Iroquois Theatre fire of 1903. At Northbrook samples of this hardware are put through 100,000 openings and closings by a Rube Goldberg device, to make certain that it does not bend under the repeated beatings it receives, and possibly freeze shut at a critical moment.

Underwriters' Laboratories tests much of the equipment used in fire protection. It puts samples of rubber used in fire hose through accelerated aging tests, by exposing them to oxygen and heat for a few days to simulate the effect of years of normal aging. Then the rubber is stretched to determine how much of its tensile strength and elongation remains after the aging.

The men who test fire extinguishers set off and extinguish one fire after another to check the effectiveness of the various chemical agents employed in fighting three basic kinds of fires: Type A, which is ordinary combustible material such as wood, cloth and paper; Type B, petroleum fires; and Type C, electrical fires. Especially important to the testers is the ease with which untrained amateurs can be expected to use the equipment. In fact, the Laboratories men add a large safety factor to the time in which they extinguish a test fire, because they know that the novice often sprays much of the chemical into the air. Even after he aims it correctly he would rarely fight the fire as effectively as the experienced fireman or a tester at Underwriters' Laboratories.

The great variety of Underwriters' Laboratories testing extends wherever it can help promote public safety. It concentrates, for instance, on the special hazards of the hospital, where electrical equipment is used in close proximity to ether and other explosive gases. Here a spark from an ordinary motor, that would not be of concern in most other places, can cause a very dangerous explosion. The Laboratories have therefore drawn up a set of standards for sparkless motors, to be used in such devices as the electrically controlled hospital bed, which might be hazardous to the patient in an oxygen tent unless special precautions are observed. Speakers from Underwriters' Laboratories often attend meetings of doctors and hospital personnel to keep them abreast of the latest research in this particular field of safety engineering. And in connection with this work UL maintains an "explosion laboratory" where electric motors that operate in explosive atmospheres are tested for their explosion-proof qualities. At certain crucial points in the tests the testers take refuge behind a thick concrete wall and observe the experiment by means of overhead mirrors.

In another part of the Northbrook station sample roofing materials, such as composition shingles, are fastened to sections of sheathing and tested for resistance to both fire and windstorm. To be listed, shingling must withstand the direct blast of a large gas flame thrower three times, a full minute each time. Then it must protect the sheathing from deep charring while a number of burning brands rest on it until they burn out. In the windstorm test, roofing shingles must withstand an edgewise sixty-five-mile blast in a wind tunnel without the edges being blown upward and roofing ripped away. This test has stimulated the development of several inventions to seal composition shingles, including methods of overlapping and of gluing the shingles to one another.

In the Steiner Tunnel Furnace, named after Albert J. Steiner of the Underwriters' Laboratories who developed it in the course of his work, engineers can test wall, floor and ceiling panels to find out three important facts about them: how quickly they transmit flame from one place to another, how much smoke they create, and how much fuel they contribute to a fire. From the tunnel furnace tests materials achieve numerical ratings from which a user can judge their fire-resistant qualities. After the disastrous La Salle Hotel fire of 1946 in Chicago, a sample section of the highly polished plywood paneling that had spread the fire with startling rapidity was tested in the tunnel furnace. It was found that this material roared into flame from one end of the tunnel to the other with amazing speed. Under the initial heat the laminations spread apart like a flower in the morning sun, not only exposing more wood surface to the air, but also exposing a highly flammable glue to the flames. On the strength of that post-mortem test, and a number of others. Underwriters' Laboratories waged a hard campaign against the practice of using flammable glues in the manufacture of plywood.

Less important to the average homeowner, but of great interest to banks and other institutions holding valuables, is the work of the Burglary Protection Department of the Laboratories. Here, over the years, have been tested many improvements in laminated, bullet-resistant glass, which must stand up under bullets fired from various weapons at fifteen feet, according to the rating sought by the manufacturer. In this department the burglary skills of two thoroughly honest lock-picking specialists of Underwriters' Laboratories have been matched against combination locks used on safes of all descriptions. The locking mechanism aside, safes and money chests are also tested for their resistance to cutting tools, burning torches and explosives such as nitroglycerine.

Recently the Laboratories have been called upon to test a great variety of burglar-alarm systems, which have been greatly improved since World War II. There are ultrasonic alarms, set off by the softest of footfalls; there are body induction alarms, triggered by the presence of a foreign body in the protected area; there are movement-detection devices—and others which manufacturers and Laboratories do not discuss in public. The greatest problem, still largely unsolved, is how to achieve stability in burglar-alarm systems, so that they are not set off by the rumbling of a truck on the street, or by a rat, or the office cat, or a careless employee. Underwriters' Laboratories will occasionally test an alarm system at night in the field. But contrary to some romantic tales that have been circulated, the police are always "in on the job" and are usually present when a UL engineer tries to penetrate the protection system being tested. The testing job is difficult enough without adding the hazard of an accidental shooting.

Perhaps the most spectacular test of all at the Laboratories is the fire-and-drop test for safes, which determines whether an office safe can protect papers while the office building burns to the ground around and beneath it. In this test the safe is roasted at 2000 degrees Fahrenheit for three hours. Then it is lifted, glowing red, to a three-story height and dropped into a pit lined with broken concrete and bricks, to simulate its fall into the basement of a burning building. If it does not burst open, it is put back into the furnace and cooked for another half-hour upside down. When the safe is finally smashed open after cooling (the combination lock is always completely ruined), the papers inside must not be scorched, or even brittle. Thousands of listed safes have protected their contents through the most intense building fires, thanks to this rigorous testing at the Chicago laboratories.

In all its tests UL is certain that all products in the same classification are given equal treatment. Furnace heats are adjusted carefully according to a standard time-temperature curve which simulates the increase in heat of a building fire, minute by minute. In all tests in which heating plays a part the most commonly observed instrument in the Laboratories is the thermocouple, which is imbedded in the material being heated and which records the temperature changes by wires that lead to a printing device. Technicians hold stop watches on materials subjected to fire for a given time; counters record the exact number of times a switch is turned or panic hardware is banged open. Even the steel ball that is swung against the television screen is held to a uniform height on a measured platform. Uniformity of test conditions is an absolute rule at the Laboratories.

There is no soliciting of clients and no advertising on behalf of Underwriters' Laboratories. Established manufacturers know them of old, and a new one learns soon enough the advantage of putting his products through testing so that he may carry the UL label. In a typical case, the manufacturer inquires into the testing program for a given product, and is told the classification in which it fits and is given a copy of the printed UL standard appropriate to it. At this point, therefore, he knows what performance Underwriters' Laboratories expects of his product and what tests it will be put through. He has time to modify his product, if he wishes, before submitting it for testing. When he is ready to proceed, he usually comes to the station for a conference and is told the maximum charge for testing his product, the nature of the Laboratories' follow-up service should it be listed, and any other relevant details. The manufacturer is invited to send a witness to the tests, and frequently one of his production engineers is right on the spot—particularly in fire-resistance tests like those run on wall paneling and safes.

On big, costly items, one sample is usually sufficient; but on smaller items, such as percolators or light switches, the Lab men may want a half dozen or even a dozen samples to examine and abuse. When the testing is all over, the manufacturer is welcome to his tested (and often ruined) samples if he will pay the freight for their return. Sometimes it is important for his engineers to study the model that failed, but in other cases a junk service hauls the wreckage from the Laboratories.

Relations between Laboratories and client do not end with listing, but continue as long as the product is listed by the Laboratories. The UL follow-up services include supplying the appropriate labels to the manufacturer, and re-examining his product periodically to insure that it remains at the same safety standard as when it was successfully tested. UL representatives make frequent visits to factories, often unannounced, to check the efficiency of the maker's own inspection system. These men are scattered across the country in hundreds of cities, wherever the inspection work load requires them. At times they buy samples on the open market, to compare them with those checked in the factory.

Should any product be found deficient, the Laboratories immediately notify the manufacturer to correct what is wrong. Until the deficiency is corrected, the product is not permitted to bear labels or other evidence of listing. Labels remain Laboratories property until an article is moved into commerce. There have been scattered instances of chiselers trying to hoodwink the inspectors with samples of higher quality than the normal production run, but they have had little success. And the few who have tried to counterfeit the UL label have been quickly apprehended and forced into court to pay damages. The fact that any of them have tried such ruses indicates how highly they prize the Underwriters' Laboratories listing and label.

The consumer, whether a housewife or a do-it-yourself purchaser of power tools, or the member of a church building committee, can easily check on a manufacturer's claim that his product is listed by the Laboratories. All he needs to do is look him up in one of the seven UL lists. The lists are in the form of booklets, of which the thickest has more than 500 pages. Each is carefully indexed. The *Accident, Automotive, and Burglary Protection Equipment List* contains, among many other things: window cleaners' belts and fittings; elevator appliances; pressure cookers; floor coating and finishing materials (for safety against danger of slipping and falling); automotive heaters, mufflers, and seat belts; burglar alarm systems, bullet-resisting materials ("bulletproof" is a misnomer), locks, and parking meters (listed as safe from pilferage).

The other six lists are somewhat more specialized. They cover products which their titles suggest, as follows: *Electrical Appliance and Utilization Equipment; Electrical Construction Materials; Building Materials; Fire Protection Equipment; Gas and Oil Equipment; and Hazardous Location Equipment.*

In addition to publishing the lists, Underwriters' Laboratories keeps in print some 200 *Standards for Safety,* each of which details the UL safety requirements for one classification of product. These Standards tell the manufacturer about the ordeals to which his products will be subjected at the Laboratories if, or when, he submits them for testing. Finally, UL cooperates with the Engineering Department of the National Board of Fire Underwriters in producing research and industry bulletins on specific fire and safety subjects, and maintains a card data service by which it can distribute data on materials and hazards in brief form to interested public and industry officials.

The UL staff has grown to more than a thousand since William Henry Merrill started it in 1893. His first colleague was William Colin Robinson, who joined him shortly after the first season of the Chicago fair. Robinson was hired by the Underwriters to examine and test acetylene generators, which had become a new and dangerous hazard in many cities since the discovery in 1892 of a method of producing acetylene gas commercially for lighting. Robinson and Merrill, both only twenty-five when the Laboratories were founded, were destined to lead and build the organization for nearly thirty years until their deaths, which occurred in 1921 and 1923 respectively. During their time and since, the Laboratories have grown steadily, to the point where in 1965 the Chicago headquarters staff, in round numbers, totaled 430, with 160 at Northbrook, 35 in New York City, 150 at Melville, New York, 90 at Santa Clara, California, and 140 full-time inspectors on follow-up service work in all parts of the country. In addition there are 340 part-time inspectors in places where the work load is lighter. The entire staff includes about 270 engineers, 30 engineering assistants, 90 laboratory technicians, plus the network of factory inspectors, clerical staff and maintenance workers. A good proportion of the staff stay with the laboratories for many years, although a fair number become safety and testing specialists at UL, then gravitate toward the companies that are Laboratories' clients and frequently return to the testing station as a manufacturer's representative.

Many of the investigations today are routine because they cover ground familiar to the staff engineers. But the product is submitted for inspection in such cases because it is one new to the sales line of the submitting company, or it has a new feature making it a model different from a similar one already tested and listed. Many of the electrical products fail the first test. Yet most of the electrical equipment on the United States market is listed by the Laboratories. When considered together, these statistics reveal how effectively Underwriters' Laboratories stands guard over hazards originating in electrical equipment.

The value of the buildings, equipment and other assets of the organization is close to seventeen million dollars. Clients are charged according to the time and materials spent on their project, and test fees range widely. The Laboratories' work load has grown by approximately 10 per cent a year over the past two decades, and there is no sign to indicate any reduction in its growth rate during the years just ahead.

One costly test held in the 1950s did not come off exactly as the Underwriters' Laboratories had hoped. This was on a sprinkler system designed for use in a bonded whisky warehouse. The problem was to determine how sprinklers should be deployed so as to afford adequate protection to a valuable stock of whisky in barrels. Distillers and engineers at the time were not sure whether the barrels of whisky, in view of its high alcoholic content, would explode in a warehouse fire. To make the test thoroughly realistic, the distillers were willing not only to provide sufficient barrels thoroughly impregnated with whisky fumes, but to fill them as well. However, officials of the Internal Revenue Service, which is responsible for collecting the federal tax on alcoholic beverages, said no.

"Perhaps," one Laboratories officer commented later, "they were afraid we would steal the stuff instead of burning it up!"

The test was finally run with denatured alcohol in the fragrant barrels instead of whisky. It proved that the barrels did not explode, and that the sprinklers acted to dilute the alcohol that poured from the damaged barrels, and thus controlled the flames.

The future of Underwriters' Laboratories will be filled with responsibilities even more serious than those of the past. As American society becomes increasingly urban, and as high values become ever more tightly concentrated in cities and in large storage facilities, the consequences of a fire's getting out of control become steadily greater. Space is at a premium in high-cost areas; finished products and materials are piled higher and packed closer together. And when fire breaks out it is not just material things that are destroyed; interruption of business and loss of good will, profits and wages amount to a very large part of the total damage. The Pentagon fire in the summer of 1959 and the fire in the Nieman-Marcus department store in Dallas at the peak of the 1964 Christmas shopping season are typical cases.

With our exploding knowledge and the swift advance of technology, new products are coming to the market so rapidly that the Laboratories do not have time to accumulate field experience, as in the past. Today a manufacturer often wants his product tested and listed by Underwriters' Laboratories at the outset. There are even times when rejection of his product for listing can cause him to abandon it at that point for he has come to realize that the UL label is closely related to a wide acceptance of his product in the market place.

Such a responsibility is a burden which the Underwriters' Laboratories shoulders with pride and humility. The confidence which manufacturers and consumers repose in the Laboratories is eloquent testimony to its splendid record of unbiased investigation, of devotion to the scientific method of inquiry. It is a monument to the vision of William Henry Merrill and the underwriters who brought him to Chicago.

The effect of Underwriters' Laboratories' operation is most difficult to assess. Because of the almost universal acceptance of its findings the Laboratories' listings assist the manufacturers in achieving the mass production and distribution of goods, which forms the basis of our domestic economy. The inspection authority finds Underwriters' Laboratories listings a useful tool in discharge of his responsibilities of protection of the public. Manufacturers who do not choose to submit certain models of their line to the Laboratories for listing, nevertheless use the Standards of Underwriters' Laboratories in designing these items. Similarly, inspection authorities who are frequently called upon to accept equipment which because of rating or other reasons falls beyond the scope of the UL coverage, use the Laboratories' Safety Standards in evaluating these items. The installer can proceed with full confidence that the product can be installed and operated in compliance with nationally recognized installation and use codes. Finally, the ultimate user of the product has reason to believe that products which are listed by the Laboratories will afford him adequate protection when properly used and maintained. It is because these benefits ultimately flow to the consumer that the Laboratories slogan "Testing for Public Safety" so aptly describes its operation in the public interest.

Since 1893 Underwriters' Laboratories has built its own great tradition. It can look confidently forward into an even greater future of public service.

IX

SCIENCE ON THE TRACK OF DANGER

At 9:30 A.M. on January 22, 1958, a tremendous explosion took place in the car switching yard of the Niagara Junction Railway in Niagara Falls, New York. The blast destroyed five railroad cars, and many more were badly damaged. In the yard was left a gaping crater measuring eighty-five feet across and sixteen feet deep.

Fortunately, no one was killed. But more than 180 people were injured in some way, several critically, and 60 of them received hospital treatment. It was sheer chance that the toll in personal injury was so low.

When the events preceding the explosion were pieced together, it appeared certain that it originated in a tank car containing 77,280 pounds of nitromethane. This is an organic chemical, one of the nitroparaffins, which is considered a "potentially explosive chemical," meaning that it has a tendency to be unstable and can be exploded by heat or shock, or a combination of the two. The nitroparaffins represent a new, rapidly expanding field of chemistry which, the manufacturers say, will one day rival that of coal-tar derivatives. They are widely used already to synthesize pharmaceuticals, dyestuffs, insecticides, rubber chemicals, photographic developers, textile chemicals and resins. It is in everyone's interest that they be shipped and handled in safety.

On the heels of the Niagara Falls explosion and a similar blast four months later near Mount Pulaski, Illinois, the Engineering Department of the National Board of Fire Underwriters undertook the responsibility to study nitroparaffins and their hazards to life and property and to report on them. Published in 1959, the research report combined what was known at the time about these potentially explosive chemicals. It was a practical booklet, discussing the properties of nitroparaffins, evaluating their explosive potential, and outlining actual explosion experiences, precautionary recommendations, bibliography and other topics.

No other organization was so well equipped to step into the breach and perform such a public service. And no activity of the National Board illustrates its public service function so clearly as this action of its Engineering Department. In effect, the department is an intelligence center that gathers and transmits information in both directions between the two worlds of insurance and technology. Being more fanciful, one might call it a "Department of Technical Analysis, Forethought and Instruction." It might even be looked upon in military terms as the roving scout in the vanguard of the insurance business, always out in front, searching ceaselessly for trouble spots, and reporting back their presence and degree of seriousness to those who follow. The people as a whole are always the beneficiary.

One function of the Engineering Department, the inspection of fire defenses of municipalities, has been described in Chapter VII. An offshoot of National Board engineering is the Underwriters' Laboratories (Chapter VIII), with which the department keeps in close touch. Equally important is the variety of other engineering activity conducted in the New York headquarters. It consists of research on fire causes, the drafting of standards and recommended safeguards, compilation of suggested codes and ordinances, technical surveys of notable disasters, and information programs of many kinds.

But the National Board engineers do not work for and with the insurance business alone. They are also called upon by other organizations and by agencies of government as technical consultants, as speakers, as contributors to publications, and as members of study committees. They are, in effect, the National Board's pool of technical experts who, by their experience and the nature of their function, know more about fire and explosion causes and fire protection than almost anyone else. For this very reason they are in demand as teachers and counselors. In making a generous proportion of the time of its salaried engineers available to other agencies, the National Board believes it is fulfilling one of its public service missions.

There is a close relation between the National Board's engineering studies into fire safety and its program of public education, by which the facts of fire safety are brought home to those in a position to use them. A striking example is the work of the Special Committee on Hospitals, set up in response to the tragic 1949 fire that destroyed St. Anthony Hospital in Effingham, Illinois, with a loss of 74 lives. The Executive Committee of the National Board immediately launched a special program to inspect every hospital in the United States to determine what could be done to lessen the loss of life from fires in hospitals and nursing homes.

By the time it was completed in 1952, the inspection program initiated by the National Board covered more than 6,800 hospitals. Cooperating in carrying it out were the fire and casualty companies, their field men and agents, hospital administrators, city authorities, the American Hospital Association, and others. The inspection turned the spotlight on the great hazard to life in converted buildings, many of them former dwellings, being used as nursing, convalescent, and old-age homes and maternity hospitals. An improvement in conditions followed. At the conclusion of the inspection program, the American Hospital Association said in a letter of commendation to the National Board:

"We shall never be able to measure the number of lives that might have been lost if inspection recommendations had not been adopted to curb at their source fires that might otherwise have resulted in panic and loss of life."

The twentieth century has seen an expansion of new technical processes in industry more rapid than in any other period in history. The pace has been constantly increasing with the development of electronics, plastics, chemicals and petroleum products, among others. Today new products are developed, patented, and put on the market at a rate unknown just a few decades ago, with the result that makers and users often do not realize the risks they run in handling them. Development and testing time is cut down; distribution is speeded up. That is why, for instance, it was possible only a few years ago for a shipment of highly flammable nylon sweaters from abroad not only to reach the retail market, but to burn fatally several small children who were wearing them before they were recalled from the stores and banned by federal law.

It is no comfort to realize that the "torch sweaters" were imports. Domestic products have been found just as dangerous in the manufacturing and in the consumer stages of the economic cycle. Small manufacturers of plastics, for instance, have suffered innumerable fires and explosions because they did not understand thoroughly what they were dealing with from a chemical standpoint. Nor can consumers rely on Underwriters' Laboratories to safeguard them from every dangerous product, because many may not be submitted for testing. For example, in October 1963 the Food and Drug Administration in Washington issued a warning that a water-repellent liquid known as "X-33," commonly sold as a sealer for basement floors and walls, was dangerously explosive and had caused several serious accidents to workmen and homeowners. X-33 was taken from the market, but only after it had caused considerable damage.

The National Board's engineering staff has stepped into the widening information gap between burgeoning technology and personal safety, and has attempted to bring the two closer together. One result is its program of publishing research reports and technical surveys, each devoted to comprehensive coverage of one topic. Typical titles of booklets in this series, available to all who may think them useful, are these:

Fire Hazards of the Plastics Industry, Hazards in Molten Salt Baths for Heat Treatment of Metals, and *Survey on Causes and Prevention of Cotton Fires.*

Other publications are aimed at natural hazards, such as the booklet showing the homeowner how to lessen or prevent damage by lightning. The old-fashioned lightning rod is still recommended by the National Board engineering staff, with documentation to convince the skeptical who think that lightning rods went out with the horse and buggy. There are also booklets on precautions to take against windstorm damage, since the insured public has been taking out windstorm coverage in rapidly increasing amounts. In part, at least, the public has been made hurricane-conscious by the United States Weather Bureau's practice of designating storms alphabetically each season with girls' names; in addition, there has been a great increase in weather news carried in the press, on radio, and television.

The lessons of a long, tragic series of hotel fires are distilled in a National Board booklet entitled *Fire Safe Hotels*. People can sleep more easily in their hotel beds at night because many builders and hotel owners have applied these lessons. The same is true elsewhere. We feel reasonably confident today that our children in school are safe from fire, and our patients in the hospital. One reason is that those in positions of authority to see that such buildings are built and kept in safe condition have been guided by such booklets as *Fire Safe Schools* and *Fire Safe Hospitals*, written for their use by engineers of the National Board. It is difficult to name a situation in industry, commerce, or public activity of any sort for which there is not a suitable guide to fire safety published by the engineers of the National Board of Fire Underwriters.

Recently one of the engineers was asked how the department becomes aware that a new research booklet or survey is needed.

"By osmosis!" he replied.

He went on to explain that information on new situations that merit an engineering study reaches the staff members almost every day. The men in the department read their trade journals—in chemical engineering, construction, architecture, mechanical engineering, electrical engineering, and many more. They attend conferences of engineers, of fire officials, of manufacturers, of builders. They therefore know what is being produced and moved in commerce. Sometimes fire officials or manufacturers will phone or write to the department to ask about a certain material, product or procedure. Is it safe? they ask, or: What should we do to make it safe?

The engineers will study the questions, seek out the answers, and reply. If the questions concern enough people, a booklet may result. Again, this time after losses have already taken place, a report may reach the engineers from the statistical center of the industry, the Actuarial Bureau, pointing out that losses have become more serious in a certain activity and asking for an engineering inquiry into the reason.

The decision on which cases, or studies, receive priority is taken by a subcommittee of the National Board Committee on Engineering, which acts swiftly because its members are devoted to keeping the department's research into fire causes abreast of newly emerging problems. The day is long past when anyone could rise in an annual meeting of the National Board of Fire Underwriters and state that he believes electricity had somehow been a "mysterious" cause of fires. Today the engineers would have already informed the underwriters of a newly isolated cause of fires, and at the same time would have conferred with other technicians outside the insurance field on ways to control it.

Inquiry and information are one part of the Engineering Department mission. The other part involves getting people to act on the strength of the knowledge already acquired and published. This is the central meaning of the codes and standards work of the National Board: taking action to prevent losses.

In the best of all possible worlds one might think that once fire and explosion dangers were known and explained, prudent men would heed the warnings, with the result that there would be virtually no more accidents from causes that are known and explained. But the rules of life and human nature do not permit such an ideal world, as history teaches and reiterates. People insist on cutting corners with safety in pursuit of speed, or profit, or personal aggrandizement—or simply for pleasure. And because human society has become so closely interdependent, so physically proximate, the public safety demands rules of conduct governing all for the security of all. In so far as safety from fire is concerned, the Engineering Department of the National Board has from its beginning been the American leader in promoting standards and rules to achieve this end.

Even before the National Board of Fire Underwriters was formally organized, in fact, an emergency meeting of representatives of New England and New York stock companies, held in New York on July 9, 1866, urged the enactment of laws to suppress the use of firecrackers. This meeting had been called in response to the concern felt by many underwriters over the conflagration that had just devastated Portland, Maine, a tragedy touched off by a firecracker. The meeting, according to a contemporary account:

"Resolved: that the underwriters here, representing the insurance capital of the country, in view of the continued destruction of property by the use of firecrackers, recommend to their respective companies to take immediate measures to secure the passage of laws against the use of them under any and all circumstances where they issue policies."

This was strong language, issuing from the heat of the immediate moment, which the National Board of Fire Underwriters has not often used since that early day in pursuing its fire-safety objectives. It has sought in somewhat milder tones to enlighten, to educate, and to persuade the community and the public to adopt safety standards. Its policy has been a positive one of seeking cooperation and compliance—rather than a negative approach of advocating bans and suppressions. This is not to say that the National Board is opposed to safety codes equipped with enforcement teeth. On the contrary, it has actively promoted for years the adoption by states and municipalities of the "Big Three" recommended codes: The National Electrical Code, the National Building Code, and the Fire Prevention Code. But most of its attention has been directed to winning voluntary adherents to the cause of fire safety.

The Engineering Department has published about sixty-five booklets in a series entitled *Standards and Recommended Safeguards.* Each booklet covers one kind of materials, equipment, or enterprise having common fire-prevention features. These standard booklets are, in effect, statements of good practice recommended by National Board engineers—how-to books on fire prevention and fire readiness. A dozen or more of the standards cover fire extinguishing appliances and auxiliary equipment, detailing the recommended frequency of inspection, how to mark it with instructions for use, where to place it, how to protect it from the elements—in short, everything the user should know. There is another group of standards on flammable liquids. No. 32, for instance, is devoted to the safe operation of a dry cleaning plant in which such fluids are used. Another group of standards on combustible solids includes a booklet on safeguarding a lumberyard from fire. There are standards on the use of gases, on explosive dust, on electrical equipment, construction and transportation facilities, such as marine terminals and aircraft hangars.

The standards have not sprung full blown from the National Board of Fire Underwriters in isolation. They are the product of conferences and committee meetings involving representatives of several other organizations, of which the over-all parent group is the National Fire Protection Association. A standard, when it reaches final form, has therefore been through the mill of examination and criticism by manufacturers, dealers, transportation experts, structural engineers, fire marshals, chemists—as well as underwriters. Light on the fire-protection problem at issue has been cast from all sides in the discussion. Then the issue boils down to this: Is the proposed standard practical, fair, and likely to be effective in controlling fire and explosion? How can it be improved?

One National Board staff member has explained the procedure of working out standards this way:

"When we find that a new standard is needed, we usually do not require further research. Nor do we ask for the moon in regard to safety, just because we represent the insurance business. We try to develop standards that will provide *reasonable* protection—not absolute protection. We want the standard reasonable because we want it to be used. Standards should be so reasonable that any conscientious operator will follow them voluntarily."

Occasionally it will even happen that an engineer from the National Board will find himself in the odd position of arguing in a technical committee against a proposed clause that seems too stringent to be practical. If it is too severe, it will be evaded or disregarded, he believes.

Standards are voluntary. They may or may not be followed. Codes, on the other hand, have the force of law where adopted. Codes are really the culmination of a chain or sequence that leads backward through standards, research, and testing. Codes consist of a set of minimal standards designed for legal adoption; they express the level of performance that an authority says *must* be achieved, rather than ideals that may be sought.

The three major codes are thick books, covering every situation within their scope. The National Building Code, which came into being as a result of construction studies following the Baltimore conflagration of 1904, now contains more than three hundred and twenty pages. It includes, in addition, a tabulation of the fire resistance ratings of more than one thousand structural assemblies (roof, wall, column, beam, etc.) of various materials, showing the length of time they withstand the standard fire tests of the Underwriters' Laboratories. The National Electrical Code, originated by the National Board but maintained now by the National Fire Protection Association, runs to nearly four hundred and fifty pages. The Fire Prevention Code, comprising regulations covering a variety of fire-prevention items such as smoking, fireworks, garages, dry cleaning plants, and flammable motion picture film, is more than two hundred pages thick.

Literally thousands of agencies and local jurisdictions have adopted the codes, in whole or in part, giving them the force of law in those places. It would be obviously impossible to calculate how many millions of dollars the National Board has saved local, state, and even federal agencies by the fact of having carried out the research, gathered the results of testing at Underwriters' Laboratories, and involved the talents of thousands of experts in developing standards and drafting codes. As in many of its other activities, the National Board here performed a service that could not have been done half so well, if at all, were it not on the scene. Even a large, well-financed city or state government might never have appropriated the money needed to draft a comprehensive building code, or an electrical code. But by developing the means of working cooperatively with industry, business and public officials, the National Board has helped in leading the science of fire-prevention engineering to a high point in America.

Despite the best fire-prevention efforts in studies, tests, education and regulation, serious fires and other disasters continually take place. Sometimes they spring from an old, familiar situation, one from which an earlier disaster has clearly pointed out the steps toward prevention. After the immediate shock of such a disaster has passed, the rhetorical question is often asked: "Will we ever learn?"

The cynical insist that "the public" is too blind or too stupid ever to learn from its errors. The more optimistic believe that people do absorb lessons from tragedy, although with pitiful slowness. The clergy, the press and community leaders utter the fervent hope, almost in the tones of a prayer, that "we"—meaning the lay public—will indeed learn.

In 1947, following the terrible fire-and-explosion disaster in the Texas City, Texas, port area, the National Board of Fire Underwriters undertook to provide the means by which thoughtful, responsible people could absorb the lessons taught by major fires and explosions such as the disaster at Texas City. It has done so by publishing a series of technical reports on each of a number of significant disasters. By the mere fact of gathering and publishing an account of exactly what happened, and analyzing the reasons for what took place, the reports lead to conclusions that practical men can accept. Each of these National Board reports winds up with a set of recommendations offering at least a minimum program for controlling the dangers that lay behind the disaster in question.

Produced by the Engineering Department after on-the-spot investigation and interviews with witnesses, the National Board's reports are published with maps and startling photographs. These reports are not "shockers. They are consistently written and edited as analytical, educational documents, rather than as propaganda. The recommendations point toward conservatively conceived reforms in regulations and procedures, not to radical changes. For here as in the rest of its engineering work the National Board recognizes the limits of its function as a private business association. In general, its approach is to answer the question arising from each disaster on which it publishes a report:

"What lessons have we learned from this experience?"

Although every important disaster is in some way similar to one that has occurred earlier, it is frequently a "first" in respect to its gravity, or the particular way it was touched off, or its impact on the community. The country had experienced numerous earthquakes, for instance, before the Alaska quake of March 27, 1964, but the fact that this was the first major one since the rapid postwar development of southeastern Alaska, with vast, spectacular destruction of property and a great emotional impact on thousands of people, put it in a class apart. Clearly, it warranted special study, since applications for earthquake insurance were bound to increase tremendously. During the second and third week after the earthquake, engineers from the National Board in cooperation with an earthquake expert from the Pacific Fire Rating Bureau surveyed the disaster area, mostly around Anchorage. Their joint report illustrated in text and in forty-one revealing pictures the extent of the damage suffered by a variety of structures, and discussed the apparent reasons why some held up and others failed. Its object was to help everyone living in earthquake zones build more soundly against this peril to their property.

It was a report full of "lessons learned." The photographs of water-front damage caused by the post-quake seismic sea waves (popularly called "tidal waves") would alone give pause to anyone thinking of building on low-lying land near the shore. Several photographs documented the instability of hollow cinder and concrete blocks under lateral earthquake shaking. Others showed the severity of damage to structures with foundations that did not hold together, and to buildings that were not firmly attached to the foundation. Still other pictures of cracking and collapsed structures built in soft-earth areas illustrated again the old engineer's rule that "a building is no better than the soil beneath it."

This National Board report can bring home to any layman who lives in an earthquake zone the need for protections that he would be wise to build into his own property. It is a graphic, powerful device of public instruction for non-technicians serving on governing bodies, school boards, and zoning agencies in areas subject to earthquake. It can be used to promote more conscientious planning in the continual urban build-up of a part of the United States that is bound to see more earthquakes in the years ahead. In fact, it may be studied with profit in all parts of the country, because damage has been caused by earth tremors in almost every state. For although a quake may be termed "an act of God," uncontrollable by human effort, man can lessen its disastrous effect on life and property. The report stresses that "by judicious selection of building sites, by designing structures for lateral loads, and by good construction practices, some of the fear and much of the tragedy attending a major earth shock can be avoided."

"The Alaska earthquake," the report says in summary, "emphasizes the importance of the adoption of an adequate building code, including provisions for earthquake-resistive design, and enforcement of the code requirements, and of giving due consideration to soil conditions at the building site, if loss of life and property is to be lessened."

The most costly fire disaster in California since the 1906 San Francisco earthquake and fire was the conflagration of November 6, 1961. This disastrous fire, fanned by a strong wind, swept through a number of brush-covered canyons and ridges in the Bel-Air and Brentwood district of Los Angeles, destroying or severely damaging 496 private houses, four school buildings and twenty other small buildings. Because the district was filled with high-value residences, the insured property losses, exclusive of automobiles, totaled an estimated $24,000,000. Fortunately, no lives were lost, but more than two hundred firemen and an unknown number of civilians suffered injuries. More than six thousand acres were swept over by the fire. After the flames were out, the blackened, crumbled walls and stark chimneys standing along the residential streets looked much like the damaged remains after the worst of the fire-bomb raids of World War II.

A three-man team of engineers from the National Board of Fire Underwriters studied the conflagration with the assistance of men from the local rating bureau and from the Los Angeles departments concerned. From their twenty-page report emerged a picture of a fire menace that was allowed to increase bit by bit over the years, through indecision and neglect in many quarters, until the moment when the elements combined to set off the gigantic and costly tinderbox. The report showed, for instance:

That during the fifteen years before the 1961 Bel-Air conflagration there had been 243 brush fires in Los Angeles and Ventura Counties, each burning 100 acres or more, and that therefore the danger of fire being spread rapidly by the gusty Santana desert winds was familiar to every thinking adult in the region;

That in brush areas of Los Angeles County, ordinances in effect for many years required a minimum clear space of thirty feet around buildings—yet the law was not enforced;

That 51 per cent of the damaged or destroyed houses were set afire by sparks and heat from burning brush, and most of the remainder from flying brands landing on roofs;

That in 77 per cent of the burned houses the roof ignited first—that many of the houses had roofs made of wooden shingles, and there was no building code requirement for fire-resistant roofing;

That wide, overhanging eaves and, in some cases, the underside of hillside houses supported on columns or cantilevered out over the slope, trapped heat and sparks, thus becoming points of ignition;

That given the extreme dryness and the pillar of burning brands and sparks carried upward by the heat, then blown by the wind over a wide area, containment of the conflagration was next to impossible.

The National Board report concluded that:

> "Even after this disaster there is evidence that few people will leave these areas; most will probably rebuild and more people will follow . . . Unless definite action is taken to correct conditions existing today, the potential for similar disastrous conflagrations will continue in such areas as the Hollywood Hills, Pacific Palisades and others."

In studying the disaster of 1961 and making its recommendations (seventeen specific points are contained in the report), the National Board went as far as the mandate of a private business organization permits. It is up to public officials and the concerned private citizen to take the "definite action to correct conditions" suggested in the report. Fortunately, there are signs that some such action has followed, in Los Angeles and elsewhere, after a disaster brought dangers that were already present to the attention of those in the critical positions of authority to do something about them. To the extent that a National Board disaster report helps carry the message of a task requiring action, it fills a pressing public need. For with rare exceptions the National Board of Fire Underwriters is the only organization that conducts a thorough investigation of many such disasters.

Had the residents and the public authorities in Los Angeles paid more attention to a National Board report issued only five years before, based on investigation of a group of fires that devastated a large wooded area just a few miles west of Bel-Air, perhaps more precautions might have been taken. The so-called "Malibu fires" of December 26–30, 1956 (really three distinct blazes that burned simultaneously, with two of them merging), furnished the National Board engineers with something resembling a Hollywood prevue of the 1961 disaster. In retrospect, these passages of the National Board's report on the Malibu fire in 1956 seem like an ironic prediction of the Bel-Air fire that followed:

> The hazard to the increasing number of homes built in areas subject to intense brush fires is emphasized by these three fires. The fuel in the natural ground cover is of such vast extent and, under conditions of low humidity and high wind, is of such near-explosive characteristics as to endanger buildings over a wide area . . . Contributing to the vulnerability of individual houses are the undisturbed natural cover that extends almost to the foundations of many, as well as a total disregard in some

instances for the influence of topography on the behavior of brush fires . . . A reasonable distance of clearing can considerably reduce the quantity of heat impinging on a house, especially those built on a slope.

A highly tragic and utterly needless disaster in 1959, on which the Engineering Department issued a twenty-page report, has led to a special National Board campaign involving the public relations and legal departments as well. This is the program to safeguard America from the menace of extra-hazardous cargoes transported by truck on the highways. So far the proportion of all trucks that carry extra-hazardous cargoes subject to accidental explosion is very small, but it is growing. Serious accidents involving them have been few; but those few have signaled the need for action, and on a national scale. The National Board seeks to contain the menace as tightly as humanly possible, rather than permit it to get out of hand.

This campaign is known so far largely to specialists; but the National Board is trying to bring home the reasons for it to a wide sector of the public. Everyone knows that highway safety today is of concern to all, since we all use the roads. Yet few have stopped to recognize that the safe transportation of extra-hazardous cargoes is not merely the business of manufacturers, shippers, drivers and police agencies. In reality, it touches everyone who shares the highways with trucks bearing cargoes that have a catastrophe potential in the event of accident. Such cargoes include explosives, radioactive materials, bacterial and virus preparations, heat-sensitive and unstable chemicals and highly toxic and extremely poisonous substances—all of which are trucked along our highways today. Properly routed and handled with the necessary precaution, they present no serious problem. But in the absence of such precautions, these cargoes are more likely to become involved in an accident. If this should happen, the result can be a catastrophe.

The peaceful town of Roseburg, Oregon, was safely asleep just after 1 A.M. on August 7, 1959. Almost no one knew that at about 8:30 P.M. the driver of a two and one-half ton van-type truck had pulled up at the curb on Pine Street, a few feet from a building and supply company warehouse, in the center of the commercial district. Having completed a 290-mile run from the Pacific Powder Company plant in Tenino, Washington, the driver had arrived in Roseburg too late to make his deliveries near the town. He checked into a hotel about three blocks away, later walked back to examine his truck at about 11 P.M., then retired. No one in the Roseburg police or fire department knew that the parked truck contained two tons of dynamite, and four and one-half tons of a blasting agent trade-named "Car-Prill," a mixture of prilled ammonium nitrate, ground nut shells, and Diesel oil.

At about three minutes after 1 A.M. a couple driving past noticed that the warehouse was on fire. They at once telephoned the fire department from a nearby filling station. Due to the fact that the warehouse contained flammable materials such as paints, lacquers, thinners and gasoline, the fire was radiating intense heat into the street by the time the first fire companies arrived and started throwing water at the building. Witnesses later said that flames were reaching the parked truck, and that smoke was issuing from the vehicle, when it suddenly exploded with a tremendous roar. In the words of the subsequent National Board report:

> It is estimated that the contents of the "explosives" truck detonated at about 1:14 A.M. Thirteen people were killed, and many others were injured as a result of the explosion. A fireball with radiating heat and flames rose to an estimated 300 feet in

the air. The entire city of Roseburg was badly shaken by the blast, and windows were broken as far as nine miles away. Earthquake-like tremors were felt seventeen miles away, and a "loud thud" was heard at a distance of thirty miles. The truck had disappeared. In its place was a crater fifty-two feet in diameter and twenty feet deep. About half of the crater was blown out of the concrete paved street, and the other half from the ground beneath the warehouse building.

The largest part of the truck recovered was a rear axle, which hit a tree over three blocks away and bounded back thirty feet to the sidewalk. The warehouse where the fire had started and many buildings in the surrounding blocks were leveled; in those that were left standing, windows were knocked out, and walls were opened exposing the interior to fire.

The sequel to the explosion was a conflagration covering seven blocks and involving about forty-five buildings, where fires were touched off by radiant heat and flaming debris scattered by the explosion. Hundreds of other buildings over a fifty-block area suffered extensive blast damage. Total property loss was estimated by the General Adjustment Bureau at more than nine million dollars. The National Board report on the Roseburg disaster cannot be read by any sensitive person without his feeling its eloquent appeal for action to prevent similar circumstances.

"With the immediate application of a few simple precautionary measures, [the report said] the outcome of this grievous mishap would have been completely different. The immediate aim of this report, then, is to bring into sharp focus the attendant problems of the many important modern-day exposure hazards and to point out that proper environmental safety for our villages, small towns and the more populous centers will only be secured through the cooperative efforts of all concerned."

In this case, the report declared, "the truck was left locked and unattended, while parked in a congested area, in disregard of the Interstate Commerce Commission Motor Carrier Safety Provisions." Not only was the fire department unaware of the presence of the truck loaded with explosives within the city, but there was no ordinance in force to require the driver to notify anyone. Further, the report stated, "proper regulation and enforcement would have prevented the overnight parking of the unattended 'explosives' truck in the congested area of the city."

A ten-point program of recommendations in the National Board report on the Roseburg disaster put in first place "the need for enactment and cooperative enforcement at state and local levels of laws and regulations covering the storage, handling and transportation of explosives and blasting agents." The fact is that laws regulating highway transport of such cargoes are spotty, and vary so widely between states and towns as to be of little practical value. Further points in the report stressed the need for approved routes for trucks carrying dangerous cargoes, so drawn as to avoid population centers where possible; programs of inspection of warehouses where dangerous materials are stored; careful study and frequent review of present safety laws; firemen training programs, covering fires involving explosives and blasting agents; and required training of drivers in special steps in handling explosives.

The Roseburg tragedy, although the most spectacular truck blast on record, was far from the first big explosion of this kind. One that occurred just three months earlier, on April 3, 1959, offers a sharp contrast to it, however, in terms of the result. A truck transporting a cargo of dynamite, blasting agent and detonating fuses near Unionville,

Ohio, caught fire when the tarpaulin covering the cargo came in contact with the hot exhaust pipe of the motor. The driver and all persons in the area withdrew to a safe location. The truck and its contents burned in an open field for almost two hours before exploding with great violence. No one was injured, but the explosion completely destroyed the truck and created a crater forty feet in diameter and twenty feet deep.

Ten years before that, by strange coincidence on Friday the 13th of May 1949 another incident involving a fire in a truck loaded with chemicals resulted in an extremely serious accident—but by the greatest of good fortune it fell short of the much more disastrous one it might have become. This was a chemical truck fire in the Holland Tunnel, the busy highway tube under the Hudson River, linking New Jersey and New York City. At the peak of the morning rush hour a trailer truck loaded with drums of carbon disulfide caught fire shortly after entering the tunnel at the New Jersey end. The burning truck halted all traffic, as smoke poured from the tunnel, and fugitives from stranded vehicles staggered from the tube. Firemen experienced great trouble breathing as they fought the blaze. Although no one was killed, sixty-six persons were injured by heat and smoke and a number of trucks caught in the fire were completely destroyed—those closest to the chemical fire being melted into shapeless masses of twisted metal. Tiling and concrete were destroyed along 600 feet of the Holland Tunnel, and traffic in this busy artery could not be resumed until nearly three days after the fire. Damage from the tunnel fire was estimated at close to $1,000,000. Authorities on the spot agreed that if the chemical load had exploded violently instead of burning, the loss of life and property might have been greatly multiplied. The casing of the tunnel might have been broken, permitting water from the Hudson River to come flooding in.

The National Board engineering report on the Holland Tunnel truck fire brought out a number of interesting background facts:

That fires in the tunnel were not uncommon, since they had numbered about fifty in the average year; only one previous fire, however, had been serious;

That the load of chemicals causing the big 1949 fire was running in violation of both Interstate Commerce Commission regulations and those of the Port of New York Authority, which operates the Holland Tunnel;

That even within the first few weeks after the fire many trucks containing large amounts of dangerous chemicals had to be turned away at the entrance of the tunnel because their loads were in violation of Port Authority regulations.

What is needed, the National Board report on the Holland Tunnel fire declared, is not more rules, but proper enforcement of present ones:

"There is a much greater need for the broadening of enforcing powers with provisions to treat serious violations as felonies, with heavier fines and stiffer imprisonment terms, rather than as ordinary misdemeanors."

All this was ten years before the Roseburg disaster. There was adequate precedent, therefore, on which the National Board in 1959 launched a nationwide campaign to alert the country to a menace that had been steadily increasing for years. Since then it has sought to enlist the aid of manufacturers of hazardous materials, trucking companies, newspaper and magazine editors, legislators, state highway commissioners and everyone else who can be reached.

Among other steps, it has drawn up a suggested guide,

or plan, for legislative action by the states, that would prescribe safety procedures covering the transportation of extra-hazardous commodities on the highways. In this printed guide are spelled out the steps that each state ought to take in its own way (the National Board emphasizes that its aim is "to promote uniformity of practice rather than uniformity of wording") to safeguard its own citizens and property from fire and explosion. The underwriters recognize that there must be a long campaign, with numerous setbacks and reverses, before this menace is defeated, as other hazards have been through the history of fire-safety engineering. An especially bad truck explosion well after the Roseburg disaster points up this fact.

Near Bushkill, Pennsylvania, on June 26, 1964, a truck trailer, parked temporarily beside the road while the driver sought a repairman, caught on fire and exploded, killing six people. It left a blast crater measuring sixty by twenty feet, and ten to fifteen feet deep. Reporting this accident in a memorandum sent to state officials in all parts of the country, Lewis A. Vincent of the National Board pointed out this ominous fact:

"For purposes of comparison, the truck which exploded here had almost two and one-half times the quantity of explosives that devastated the central section of Roseburg."

Fifteen tons of explosive carried in one truckload on the public highway in 1964! Containing a rolling danger of this magnitude is, indeed, a major task for the National Board of Fire Underwriters, undertaken in the public interest. It is a situation that will probably become worse before it gets better. Yet it will be surmounted in the end, if the history of the National Board proves anything, because a validly conceived campaign, when stubbornly pursued, eventually finds acceptance among the thoughtful people who count in any civilization.

An example of a long campaign conceived and pushed by the Engineering Department for years was the drive to bring about a national standard in screw threads for fire-hose couplings and fittings. In the early days of American fire fighting it did not much matter that fire hose couplings in various cities and towns were equipped with threads of whatever size the city specified. But in the great Boston fire of 1872 firemen were unable to use some of the equipment rushed in from neighboring towns because it did not fit the city outlets. There was spasmodic discussion of standardizing fire-hose threads during the next three decades, but since only a handful of specialists could work up any interest in the topic, little was done.

Then came the Baltimore fire of 1904, to which equipment was brought by train from Washington, Wilmington, Philadelphia, and New York. Much of the "foreign" apparatus was utterly useless, however, because the other cities did not have fire hose with threads on the Baltimore standard. Some ingenious New York firemen managed to use part of their equipment by opening hydrants, running the water into open pits, then drafting water from that source. The lesson—one national standard screw thread for fire-hose couplings and fittings—fairly cried out from the ruined commercial heart of Baltimore. The National Board took up the issue in all seriousness, and working closely with other groups in the National Fire Protection Association, printed pamphlets and sent out speakers to promote the cause of standardization.

The first fifteen years were the hardest. The idea and the machinery were there, but progress in terms of actual results was slow until the spring of 1919, after World War

I. Then the doctrine of fire-hose standardization began to catch on rapidly, and the twenties saw the first wide-scale acceptance of the standard by city after city. The test by fire came in the conflagration that struck the mill city of Fall River, Massachusetts, on February 2, 1928. Twenty-three neighboring cities and towns responded to the Fall River alarms, with a total of thirty-five pieces of apparatus. A report drawn up by the National Board after the fire contains this testimonial to the value of its standardization drive:

> Three years ago [in 1925] Fall River had hose and hydrant coupling dimensions of 3-inch outside diameter and 8 threads to the inch; all surrounding cities and towns, except Newport, had the Roxbury thread of 3 1/16-inch outside diameter. With the cooperation of the then New England Insurance Exchange, all couplings on hose, apparatus, and equipment were changed to the National Standard, with 3 1/16-inch outside diameter and 7 1/2 threads to the inch.
>
> Thus all the aiding companies were able to connect to Fall River hydrants and to use hose carried on any apparatus except the companies from Newport, which brought and used adapter couplings. The value of standardized hose and hydrant couplings was outstanding, as the aid from other departments was a large factor in stopping the conflagration.

After Fall River the campaign picked up momentum. By 1940 a compilation made by the National Board showed that all cities of 20,000 population or more in sixteen states and the District of Columbia had adopted the National Standard couplings, and many cities in the other states had done so. In the past quarter century even more progress has been made, yet the campaign continues. Today the nonstandard equipment, in almost every place where it remains, is backed up by adapters that permit its use on National Standard outlets. This is a positive achievement in public protection, in which the National Board of Fire Underwriters has played a major part. Yet few laymen realize that the gauge of fire hose and couplings in their town was ever an issue.

There is never any lack of new problems demanding attention from the Engineering Department. They spring from the very dynamism of the American economy, technology and architecture. Suburban supermarkets and other large structures of modern design, with tremendous expanses of undivided space, have only lately brought forward the issue of containing a fire, once started, to prevent its destroying the entire premises. The shopping center that has grown on the outskirts of the city presents an entirely new dimension in fire fighting to a residential community that may never have experienced a large-building fire. The trend toward large, flat roofs brings with it the danger that petroleum-based roofing materials when heated by a fire at one point may melt and pour fuel directly into the hot spot as the roof buckles under the heat. (This happened with a vengeance at the Livonia, Michigan, General Motors plant fire in 1953.) Or fire fighters may reach a burning windowless building quickly, then be forced to waste valuable time smashing a hole through which to play the hose stream on the fire.

In their incipient stages now, but looming large ahead, are the problems involved in safeguarding electronic computers and data processing systems. Here is tremendous electrical potential, and records of great value stored and processed in a small place. The $20,000,000 Pentagon fire of 1959, which largely destroyed electronic equipment and the tape vault containing six or seven thousand reels of records, served warning of what can happen on a larger scale unless the danger of fire is controlled. The same is true of the few (and unpublicized) accidents to date involving radioactive materials and rocket fuels. National Board engineers have assisted in post-accident studies in these cases and will doubtless be called upon to render such service in the years ahead.

In the field of atomic energy, the National Board has provided the vehicle by which the insurance business organized a pool to participate in the huge risk of insuring commercial properties making use of nuclear power. When the atomic age dawned at the end of the second World War, there was no operating experience in industrial use or any sound actuarial basis of past losses on which companies could rely to insure safely a property using atomic energy. Consequently, government at first provided much of the insurance. After the National Board had studied the performance of atomic installations, and evaluated the potential hazards, the Board drew up a program under which the companies could set up an underwriters' pool. Now the insurance business is increasing its participation in the financial protection needed in the nuclear era.

Yet even as they devote themselves to such sophisticated aspects of safety from fire and explosion, National Board engineers still hammer away at the basic lessons. For still the home, the workshop, the store, and factory of traditional design is where most fires start, as they have since the Engineering Department undertook its labors.

X

WHEN CATASTROPHE STRIKES

EVERY WEEK or two in late summer and fall a tropical storm gathers force several hundred miles out to sea from the southeastern coast of the United States and starts moving toward the continent. It is typical of many disturbances picked up in the hurricane season by the instruments of the United States Weather Bureau. As the storm watchers broadcast warnings of the coming blow to the people living in its path, property owners do what they can to prepare against it. They beach their small craft, put outdoor furniture under cover, remove portable items from low-lying areas, and board up windows that face the rising wind.

Yet long before those in the path of the storm have begun to take these emergency steps in their own defense, insurance industry men both near and far away have already been preparing to come to their aid as soon as the fury of the storm shall have passed. For immediately after the physical safety of people, the prompt provision of money for repairs is the most pressing need of those in a community stricken by catastrophe. When the wind dies away and the high waters recede, nothing is more important to the property owner than getting his loss claim paid. Insurance company checks are the sole guarantee that damaged property will soon be made whole again.

When 50,000 insured property owners all demand attention at once from the insurance adjusters in a limited locality, chaos is the inevitable result. Rather, it *was* the result until the National Board of Fire Underwriters evolved its Catastrophe Loss Adjustment Plan.

In essence, the catastrophe plan is a nationwide system of preparation and procedures, supported by the insurance business, under which men and money are poured rapidly into the breach. Its purpose is to organize the quick and fair payment of policyholders' claims under conditions which otherwise would be frustrating, even maddening, to almost everyone concerned. It is a plan to bring order in an extraordinarily upsetting situation, to provide true information with which to counter rumor, and to prepare a list of current prices on materials and labor so that adjusters called into the area may be guided by local costs of repairing and rebuilding.

The National Board's Catastrophe Loss Adjustment Plan, as its name suggests, centers on the insurance adjuster. He must play the key role in settling any insurance claim, because he deals with the assured personally on behalf of the company. The adjuster inspects the property damage, discusses the loss with the policyholder, and assists him in preparing his loss form. Normally, as in the case of a single fire, or storm damage to a few houses, the adjuster can accomplish his task within a few days of receiving word of the loss. But in the wake of a hurricane disaster, or a great conflagration, he would be swamped under a number of adjustment calls perhaps exceeding his work load for the entire previous year. If property owners are not to be kept waiting for an unreasonable time, therefore, the adjusters in a stricken place must for a while receive outside help. The Catastrophe Loss Adjustment Plan encourages and promotes arranging in advance for enough additional adjusters to come in, and organizes their smooth, efficient settling of thousands of claims in the shortest possible time.

Well before a tropical storm has boiled out of the Atlantic or the Gulf of Mexico and has done its first damage on the United States coast, members of the Adjustments Department of the National Board in New York have been following its course with close attention. On a large chart they pinpoint with a little red flag each identifiable storm center that the Weather Bureau indicates is heading toward this country. An arrow is set on the chart alongside the flag, pointing in the direction in which the storm has been moving, and marked with its apparent speed. As radio and telephone reports come in from the Weather Bureau, flags and arrows are moved accordingly. When a marker reaches a critical point that indicates where and when the storm will probably strike the United States, the general adjuster of the National Board makes telephone contact with area and national adjusters' organizations to prepare to cooperate in emergency adjustment work on a broad scale.

The message from New York is often nothing new to the insurance organizations operating in the path of the oncoming storm. For some years now the National Board, in cooperation with state and local insurance organizations, has been laying the groundwork for just such emergency operations. They have done so in numerous ways: through conferences in which adjustment procedures following other catastrophes have been put through a "post-mortem" analysis; by appointment of emergency adjustment plan committees; and, most important, by distributing printed matter explaining the plan for catastrophe loss adjustment. If every insurance man does not know his job at least in a general way, the material is at hand by which he can quickly become educated. In this way the machinery is usually ready for emergency action even before a hurricane smashes the first window in a beach-front cottage.

The pre-disaster groundwork has been prepared most soundly in the states fronting on the country's Gulf and Atlantic coasts, from Texas around the curve of the Gulf shore to Florida, and thence north to New England. This is the sector where the threat of incoming hurricanes has been repeated so often in the past twenty years that the emergency adjustment machinery is almost as well prepared as that of a fire company to fight a fire. Beyond this coastal strip the plan has been explained to insurance men everywhere else, because no part of the country is immune to catastrophe. Severe wind, hailstorm, tornado, conflagration, or earthquakes have in the past visited great damage in almost every state of the Union. Because such a catastrophe may be a once-in-a-lifetime experience, most people are unprepared for it. That is why the National Board Adjustments Department is ready to go anywhere in the country, at any time it is needed to serve the policyholders and the insurance business.

In the *Catastrophe Loss Adjustment Procedure,* a booklet which is the National Board's basic medium for informing insurance men in all sectors of the business how the plan works, the philosophy of the plan is said to start:

. . . with the premise that a catastrophe is everybody's business and that all desire to accept freely their share of the problems, temporarily laying aside routine procedure and individual advantage.

"Laying aside routine procedure" is, in fact, the heart of the matter. Routine adjustment procedure breaks down in a catastrophe. Business as usual is just not good enough at such a time. The role of the National Board Adjustments Department is that of advance planner and coordinator of the extraordinary services that the situation demands. In no sense, however, does the National Board move in as a "take-over" group that gives orders in the adjustment of catastrophe losses. It is helper and coordinator, not master.

One of the department's first activities is to send a representative to the catastrophe scene to survey the extent of the damage. Together with men from the local adjusters' organization, the National Board representative tours the area to obtain firsthand information. After this he discusses the situation with local insurance interests in order to obtain a composite picture of the over-all insured damage involved in the catastrophe, both as to the amount of loss and the likely volume of claims. These estimates, which are relayed through the New York office, are disseminated to all companies concerned, to assist them in calculating their own involvement and the man power required. The Adjustments Department staff, highly experienced in sizing up such situations, can reach a reasonably close estimate within a few hours. On the strength of the staff member's report of estimated insured damage, and his on-the-spot recommendations, the Disaster Committee of the National Board meets to decide whether or not to authorize setting up a supervisory office to coordinate the settlement of claims. In less serious situations it might elect to open an advisory office, to assist on a more limited scale. Committee members in or close to New York generally come to such an emergency meeting on short notice; more distant members are consulted by telephone.

Depending on the severity of the adjustments problem resulting from the catastrophe, the staff and committee can decide upon various courses of action. They may find that what was feared in advance would be a serious catastrophe has turned out to be relatively minor damage, and that the adjustment load, though well above normal in the affected area, is not so great as to require special help from the National Board. In such cases a few companies facing an excess of adjustments beyond the capacity of their own staff may simply dispatch extra men to the trouble spot for a few weeks to expedite paying claims to their policyholders. If the catastrophe has run up more than one million dollars within one state in insured property damage covered by all companies, whether or not members of the National Board, but excluding marine and inland marine losses involving moving cargoes, and automobile losses, the general adjuster recommends the assignment of a catastrophe serial number to the entire event, to identify the losses under it as coming from this common source. The number helps later in the actuarial study of losses from each catastrophe that can lead (as seen in Chapter IV) to fresh insights into ways with which to handle them.

Simultaneously with assessing the amount of damage from a given catastrophe, the adjustments staff determines how it is to be handled. Several times in each year, on the average, it is decided that the National Board should open a supervisory office to coordinate the adjustment of a great many claims concentrated within a limited area. One might consider this the "full service" of the National Board in a catastrophe situation. In the case of a hurricane where there has been advance warning, this full service is under way even before the storm strikes.

A standard poster entitled "STORM PRECAUTIONS," prepared and circulated by the Insurance Information Institute in cooperation with the National Board, may already have appeared in the local press as a public service advertisement. The Institute may also have arranged for broadcast spot announcements, containing the same information, over radio and television. Precise and explicit without being overly cluttered with confusing detail, "STORM PRECAUTIONS" is a brief, practical instruction sheet explaining, among other things:

... how you can help protect yourself, your family and your property in the event that the hurricane should hit this area. These precautionary measures are suggested by the National Board of Fire Underwriters on the basis of many years of experience in the observance and analysis of hurricane damage.

There follow several paragraphs telling the public to get away from beaches and the low water front, to store loose material and porch furniture under cover, to raise movable awnings or remove them entirely, to fasten down shutters securely, to fasten exposed garage doors particularly well, to draw an emergency supply of fresh water, to open a window on the lee side to allow high wind pressure to escape—and so forth. No other agency, public or private, prepares and disseminates so much practical guidance for the protection of the public.

A series of leaflets and advertisements for use immediately after the storm is already provided to the press and other news outlets. Sometimes leaflets bearing the same message have been distributed door to door by the Boy Scouts or members of other civic organizations. The purpose of these announcements is to satisfy the natural curiosity of the insured public, just as quickly as possible, that their claims will be taken care of. For even as the storm is ebbing from its peak fury, insurance agents are being swamped with messages from their clients that they are making damage claims under their insurance policies. If the telephones are in working condition, the lines into insurance agents' offices are jammed. At best the harried agent can only promise to get an adjuster to the property as soon as possible.

Under the catastrophe plan, one of the first steps taken by the National Board staff representative is to secure an emergency headquarters for the supervisory office, perhaps in a business building, a hotel or a vacant store. He sees to it that an adequate supply of standard adjustment forms are on hand (there are times when a National Board staff member brings them with him by plane from New York), and that emergency telephone lines are run into the supervisory office. Key people in the news media are informed of these steps, to the end that they can get the reassuring word out to the public that help is being organized. One of the first messages they are asked to stress is that the adjusters have been urged to give priority to the most severe hardship cases, such as the repair of serious damage to the roof of a house sheltering a bedridden invalid or a baby.

Other points which the National Board seeks to convey directly to the people as soon as practical are:

Property owners should report damage to their own independent insurance agent who, pursuant to instructions from the company, will report it to a qualified adjuster;

Additional adjusters are being rushed to the catastrophe area, or have already arrived, and are moving as fast as possible to settle everyone's claim; therefore, please be patient; and,

It is to your interest to make every possible effort to protect your property from further damage. Make what temporary repairs you can where necessary to prevent further damage.

Through years of experience with storm claims, insurance companies have encountered widespread misunderstanding of provisions relating to water damage. Many policyholders have revealed when making claims after a catastrophe, or a lesser storm, that they did not know about the water damage exclusions in their policies. In an effort to help the insured and the underwriters understand one another, the National Board has published a special leaflet for distribution in such situations. It urges the insured to read their policies with special attention to exclusions, in order to avoid misunderstanding or disappointment. The National Board message says:

> One of the exclusions in practically every policy concerns certain types of water damage. This exclusion states that the policy does not cover damages caused by any of the following hazards:
>
> Flood, surface water, waves, tidal water or tidal wave, overflow of streams or other bodies of water, or spray from any of the foregoing, whether driven by wind or not.
>
> This exclusion is standard for property insurance policies except in rare instances.

The National Board message goes on to state that:

> It has always been the policy of America's Capital Stock Insurance Companies to be fair and reasonable in the settlement of all property damage claims filed by policyholders. In situations where the nature or cause of the damage is question-

able, every effort is made to give the insured the benefit of the doubt.

Within three days of the occurrence of a disaster the emergency machinery is usually ready to start processing claims with dispatch and yet with a high degree of accuracy and attention to the details of each case. Indeed, it is much in the interest of the underwriters that the adjustments be accurate; otherwise, haste in closing cases would only make for waste. And the waste would be largely of the insured public's money. For while property owners want speed in settling their claims, their long-range interest demands that their own adjustments and those of their neighbors be fair ones, in accordance with the terms of the insurance contract. Loss experience in any jurisdiction is always finally reflected in insurance rates. In consequence, every buyer of insurance has an interest, whether he recognizes it or not, in preventing a widespread overpayment of claims.

One of the first tasks of the local disaster committee is drawing up what the National Board calls an "advisory price list," which outlines current labor and materials costs for repair work in the area. If the local organization has prepared well before the catastrophe, it already has a list of prices representing normal charges by contractors in the region for the standard jobs.

This work by local disaster committees, organized by the National Board of Fire Underwriters, and sometimes aided by community officials outside the insurance business, has saved property owners untold millions of dollars. It has, in effect, proved that when one well-prepared group takes the initiative, it can organize the repair of catastrophe damage at prices that are reasonably close to those in a normal, competitive situation.

There is nothing compulsory about the price list; it is, as its name implies, advisory. In some areas the list may carry more than twenty-five kinds of roofing, for instance, and include such other items as removal of the old roof, installations of gutters, flooring, siding, Celotex, exterior and interior painting, floor sanding and finishing, brick-work, millwork, screens, and cleaning terrazzo floors. Prices are usually listed for material "in place," which includes labor and a reasonable contractor's profit.

Simultaneously with distributing information to the anxious public in the catastrophe area, organizing an advisory office, and setting up an advisory price list, the general adjuster of the National Board has been recruiting a corps of special catastrophe adjustment supervisors to go to the scene by the first possible transportation. One member of the National Board adjustment staff is always present. Joining him are a number of men chosen from the Adjustments Department's man power pool, many of them only recently retired from full-time employment with companies and bureaus, who are free to travel and who are still in their prime. The priority list of twenty-five adjusters on call for catastrophe work includes some of the finest talent in the insurance business. A number of these men have been vice presidents of major insurance companies. In case of need, the general adjuster has two additional panels of experienced adjusters to backstop the first twenty-five men.

On assembly in the catastrophe area, the out-of-state adjustment supervisors usually attend an orientation class to acquaint them with special practices and conditions of the locality. Then they go to work in the newly opened National Board supervisory office, going over the loss forms as they flow in. The general adjuster's rule of thumb calls for the majority of the loss to be cleaned up within sixty to ninety days. Often the task is finished much more quickly. One good adjuster should handle some two hundred losses in a ninety-day period. This figure, which is an average, should permit him enough time to give each claim proper attention without lingering over the settlement. If the National Board had not organized the system under which he was brought to the disaster site, property owners seeking payment would have had to await payment for several long months in many cases.

The skilled adjuster's presence in a stricken area benefits the assured in another way—by getting the adjustment correct the first time. Too often in the past property owners have been led to believe that their claim had "gone through" and they will receive payment, only to find that the adjuster did not do his job to the satisfaction of the underwriter concerned. Many independent adjusters are highly skilled professionals of impeccable character, who pitch in to help shoulder to shoulder with the company and bureau men and the visiting group from the National Board staff. But in a community stricken by catastrophe there is always pressure exerted on the adjusters to work at top speed, and sometimes this leads to numerous errors in loss forms. One of the purposes of the National Board in setting up its advisory office is to control this sort of haste. It does so by arranging that each adjuster working in the emergency fill out a detailed registration form, by providing for the adjuster's signature on each loss claim, by requiring him to state that he made a personal inspection of the damage, with date, and other such steps.

Claims are then checked by the supervisory office, to which they are funneled by the many adjusters at work in the stricken area. From the errors and discrepancies between claims that the supervisory office turns up, the companies are alerted to the most oft-repeated deficiencies in their adjustment work. Like several other services of the National Board this is one that no single company could afford to do thoroughly alone, especially in the rush of work following a catastrophe, but which the business as a whole can carry out through its trade organization.

Through its catastrophe plan the National Board strives for prompt and fair settlement of every legitimate claim. This is what the public rightly expects from the insurance business. The catastrophe procedure manual lists under the duties and responsibilities of adjusters:

> ... making sure there is a clear understanding that all reasonable doubt, both as to questions of coverage and amount of loss, should be resolved in the policyholder's favor.

It goes on to say:

> To underpay a loss is as evil as to overpay a loss. However, we must not forget that the policyholder who does not have a loss has rights to be preserved just as much as does the policyholder who has a claim under his insurance policy. Premiums inevitably reflect the loss experience.

The problem of handling a tremendous number of adjustments at one time vexed the insurance business for many years before the present plan was worked out. Before 1938, however, the problem did not reach the proportions it has today because the number of homeowners carrying hurricane and windstorm coverage, beyond the basic fire insurance policy, was relatively small. Then in September 1938 the fickle forces of nature taught the heavily populated northeastern section of the country a terrible lesson. An Atlantic hurricane of great destructive force ripped across Long Island and tore northward through the heart of New England. The region had never seen such devastation. People became storm-damage conscious.

At the next annual meeting of the National Board, held in May 1939, the report of the Committee on Adjustments indicated that the pattern of the future—preparation for such a catastrophe in advance—was already in evidence in primitive form. The committee's report on the 1938 New England hurricane stated:

History of that event will record that property values destroyed actually exceeded those which were consumed in the San Francisco conflagration. Although the loss to insurance was by no means as extensive, on account of the belief that the Northeastern Seaboard was immune to destructive wind storms, the problem of adjusting a vast multitude of claims was greatly complicated by the temporary breakdown of facilities for transportation and communication.

Within the shortest possible space of time your Committee met with a committee of the Eastern Loss Executives Conference and outlined an orderly procedure for the prompt and efficient adjustment of claims which were anticipated. Steps looking to the employment of emergency equipment of the National Board were immediately taken and, as a result, the adjustment of more than 27,000 claims, amounting in the aggregate to nearly $10,000,000, was greatly expedited.

In the wake of the 1938 hurricane property owners who had been forced to finance their own rebuilding and repair work began to buy windstorm insurance in great volume. In September 1944 another storm swept up the Atlantic seaboard, leaving widespread damage behind. Although total losses were less than those caused by the 1938 hurricane, insurance payments were nearly double those of six years before. In the meantime the Committee on Adjustments had been planning a more ambitious system of aid in catastrophe. The wartime man-power shortage and other stringencies prevented the full development of the "Plan for Handling Catastrophe Losses," as it was then termed. But by December of 1946 a new, improved plan had emerged from the committee. It received a thorough test in April 1947 in Texas City, Texas, when a large section of the port city was laid waste by two ship explosions and widespread fires. A National Board supervisory office set up in Texas City cleared nearly four thousand individual claims in two months. This situation was made especially difficult by the number of deaths among the insured, with the consequent necessity of carrying out adjustment with heirs. In September of that same year supervisory offices again proved their effectiveness in speeding settlement of claims from a hurricane that struck the Florida, Mississippi and Louisiana coastline. Three offices, in Miami, in Gulfport, Mississippi, and in New Orleans, handled 77,202 claims for more than twenty-one million dollars arising from this storm.

Since the busy year 1947 the Catastrophe Adjustment Plan has been steadily improved and modernized on the basis of each year's experience. Much improvement, of course, has come from the one fact of establishing an emergency plan of operation among the insurance men in each state and major urban area. Agents and adjusters are now prepared to work with far greater efficiency than before in a catastrophe, even without help from the National Board.

It is frequently the case that a catastrophe, although involving a great dollar volume of destruction, is not one where a supervisory office can be of much help. An example is the spectacular and costly fire disaster of 1961 in the swank Bel-Air–Brentwood section of Los Angeles. The insured loss was close to twenty-five million dollars, a gigantic sum, but the number of property owners affected was only a few hundred. Their claims could be handled by the adjustment man power available locally. Full-page advertisements were placed in three Los Angeles daily newspapers, however, to acquaint the policyholders with the procedure to be followed in reporting their losses, and with the plans of National Board member companies for adjusting those losses.

Another case of major catastrophe in which the disaster plan was not fully invoked was the Alaska earthquake of March 1964. Most of the Alaska destruction was not covered by insurance because residents of the affected area had not chosen to obtain it, even though it was available. Other damage close to the shore was caused by post-earthquake waves, a hazard against which coverage was not offered. The lessons of the past have been learned, however, and the insurance business expects that many property owners will seek earthquake coverage in reaction to the 1964 quake in the same understandable way that those in the northeastern states added windstorm protection to their fire policies after the 1938 experience.

The Adjustments Department rarely seems to have a typical year, the vagaries of Nature's forces being so unpredictable. March to June are the months when hailstorms and tornadoes are most frequent; September through November is the season for tropical hurricanes. Between them are lull periods, relatively speaking. But from year to year the call for catastrophe help shows no regular pattern. In some years catastrophe work occupies 75 per cent of the Adjustments Department's time, whereas in other years it may be only 25 per cent. In 1953 the National Board issued fifteen catastrophe numbers and operated six supervisory offices, four of them simultaneously. Thirteen of the fifteen catastrophes (most of them tornadoes) were bunched between March 13 and July 1. There were no numbers assigned to hurricanes in 1953. Yet the very next calendar year the Atlantic Coast states were struck by three devastating hurricanes named

"Carol," "Edna," and "Hazel" by the United States Weather Bureau, between August 30 and October 16. Estimated loss payments in these three blows ran to $265,000,000. Following these two bad years, however, the National Board did not need to open a catastrophe supervisory office until 1959.

Because no one can foretell when or where a hurricane, tornado, windstorm or hail will strike, the Adjustments Department of the National Board has striven to perfect its system of being on the alert to render catastrophe aid any time, anywhere. The plan has proven itself time and again. But the Adjustments Committee and National Board staff are constantly looking ahead to ways of improving their service to victims of disaster.

Quite separately from the adjustment of catastrophe losses, the Adjustments Department of the National Board and its governing committee have worked out methods for seeing to it that the insured is paid his claim promptly, even though there may be a disagreement among several companies over the degree of liability of each. This can occur when overlapping insurance on a given piece of property is divided among a number of policies. Formerly the policyholder in such cases had to wait a tedious time before it was agreed how much of the total claim each company was to pay. Now, however, the insured is paid at once. The companies then work out among themselves the degree of liability of each according to a code of guiding principles, the details of which need not concern the policyholder. In establishing and following this code of guiding principles for settling such cases, the National Board has improved the service of all member companies to the insured public. Most policyholders are not even aware that such a system has been set up in their interest.

Within the past few years the Adjustments Department

has become concerned with a new problem, arising from a technological development of the jet age. There has already been a trickle of claims from so-called "sonic boom," which is the shock wave sent out by aircraft flying faster than the speed of sound. Such claims can become much more frequent if large, supersonic bombing planes and commercial airliners fly regularly over the United States without precautions being taken to control the sonic boom which they cause. Many technological innovations in the past have taken place before the dangers of them were manifest. Supersonic flight differs from this pattern; the sonic boom problem is recognized by all concerned—airlines, the military, government, the public. In general, those advocating the development of supersonic flight by big planes over built-up areas are attempting to find ways to control the sonic booms to the point where they will be acceptable and manageable.

The insurance industry, however, is looking into the problem from a somewhat different angle. The designers of aircraft may succeed in curbing sonic booms to the point where most people will live with them, without damage to their nervous stability and general health. But frequent and widespread sonic booms may nonetheless lead to large numbers of damage claims for cracked window glass and plaster. The first question that arises is whether the property owner actually has coverage for sonic boom damage. As in the case of water damage, there is a great deal of misunderstanding over this point, and only certain types of policies clearly cover this hazard.

Assuming there is coverage, a second question arises: Who will pay for the damage? And how can an insurance adjuster be certain that the cracks in windows and walls shown to him by a policyholder were genuinely caused by supersonic planes? There is a danger that if damage claims based on sonic booms are paid on a broad scale, a great deal of plaster and glass damage that is due to other causes will be ascribed to sonic booms. The claims situation could become so difficult that underwriters might be forced to exclude sonic boom damage specifically from protection, or else raise premium rates to cover not only all sonic boom damage but also anything that looks pretty much like it.

The Adjustments Committee of the National Board of Fire Underwriters was on top of the problem long before most people had begun considering it. As early as September, 1953, the committee considered the matter of what it then termed "concussion damage from jet planes," specifically military planes in California. It was pointed out that on the West Coast the vehicle-damage provision of the extended coverage endorsement did not require, as in the eastern and middlewestern states, that damage be caused by "actual physical contact." The report continued:

> Whereas this situation is now confined to the operation of military jet planes, it will not be long before commercial jet planes will be in common use. It was recommended that a subcommittee be appointed to give careful consideration to the entire subject, with a report to come forward as soon as possible.

More than a decade later, from February to July 1964, the Federal Aviation Agency conducted a sonic boom experiment with Oklahoma City as the target. The FAA's purpose was to determine, if possible, what would be the effect on the city, and particularly on its people, of frequent exposure to sonic booms. Light Air Force planes were used to create the sounds and shocks. FAA staff members observed the effects of damage on a number of test buildings, and conducted interviews with local residents. The gist of the FAA's findings was that Oklahoma City could and did "take" the sonic booms.

The National Board Adjustments Department, which

kept a close eye on the experiment, remained concerned over the immense claims potential from sonic booms. During the Oklahoma City experiment some nine thousand claims were made in six months alleging damage caused by the experimental supersonic overflights. The FAA wound up paying just a few hundred claims. Members of Congress representing the unpaid property owners had the problem of satisfying them dumped in their laps.

The same sequence of events took place in Chicago a few months later, when the Air Force conducted an exercise involving many planes flying at supersonic speed over the city. An appreciable number of windows were allegedly broken and widespread cracking of walls and ceilings was reported. The Air Force promised to pay for all damage and put six adjusters on the job in the Chicago area to handle claims. But many property owners were left with claims unsettled, and congressional offices heard from them, as in the Oklahoma situation.

The solution of the problem is not yet clear. But as the experts and political authorities move toward a solution the Adjustments Department of the National Board is keeping in close touch with developments. Its aim is to see that all pertinent information relative to a new branch of technology is made available to the insurance underwriter. In this its mission is in keeping with the long tradition of the National Board, under which the use of electricity, new chemicals, plastics, building materials and many other things has been reviewed in the interest of safety to life and property. The sonic boom, however, requires control before the damage is done, rather than after, because of the possible consequences.

XI

CONTINUING THE CAMPAIGNS IN THE PUBLIC INTEREST

IT IS to the ordinary, everyday American, the man in the street, the housewife at home, the child in school and at play, that the National Board directs its continuing campaign against fire. There is a limit to what the fire departments, the engineers, and the public authorities can do to reduce the country's annual billion-dollar fire bill. Beyond that limit lies the brunt of the battle, which must be borne by everyone. To the degree that the people as a whole bring care and common sense to their activities each day, so much will be gained to the benefit of all. On the other hand, every fire loss that takes place because someone was uninformed, or careless, or lazy, impoverishes our entire society. For eventually the people pay the full fire bill through one subtle increase after another in the cost of living. Whether we know it or not, we are all paying now for the fire losses of the years just past.

The Public Relations Committee of the National Board of Fire Underwriters carries on a consistent campaign of fire-safety education. Its purpose is to inform as many people as it can reach with certain basic principles of fire safety. The National Board believes that an informed public can protect persons and property from fire far better than if all the thinking is left to others. The department's primary message is fire prevention. But it also tries to teach people the right way to handle the situation after a fire has broken out.

In 1963 the National Board supplied more than twenty-six million pamphlets, folders, and other literature requested by others for use in fire-prevention campaigns in all parts of the United States. This printed matter ranges widely in subject matter and manner of presentation. There are picture publications of the comic-book type used by school children. There are pamphlets for the adult homeowner, illustrating and emphasizing the most common fire dangers in the ordinary family house. There are special-purpose booklets, aimed at farmers, at industrial plant managers and employees. There is literature on electrical wiring, on heating systems, on special precautions to be taken at Christmas time, and even a set of fire-safety suggestions for parents dealing with baby sitters. Constantly alert to the responsibility it has undertaken in this form of public education, the National Board issues new publications as the demand dictates.

One of the most popular forms of public education on fire safety undertaken by the National Board is its motion-picture program. Any school or organization may borrow and exhibit some thirty sound films produced for the National Board by professional film makers. Their quality is attested by the many awards and citations which are proudly displayed with other testimonials of the Board's services in the public interest. The pictures, many of them in color, range in running time from five to forty-five minutes, and in subject matter from the most elementary, for the youngest school children, to the level of industrial plant supervisors, city officials, and fire departments.

Penelope Changes Her Mind, an animated cartoon that has proved very popular with primary school children, teaches the lesson of "the fire triangle" essential for combustion—oxygen, heat, and fuel. On a considerably higher level a beautifully executed scientific color film for senior high school students entitled *The Science of Fire* teaches the same fundamental fire-safety lesson. But it does so in the chemical and physics terms of the science student and adult.

The National Board picture *Heroine of the Week* is ostensibly aimed at girl "baby sitters." But the target of the message is not only the baby sitter, but also the parent who leaves her in charge of the house and younger children.

Other outstanding pictures in the National Board film library include *The First Five Minutes,* which stresses the need for having more people in industrial plants trained to fight a fire at its outset; *Are You Sure?* which reveals the emotional impact a plant fire has on five employees, each of whom thinks back to his own careless act that might have caused the fire that destroyed his work place; and *Three Strangers in Town,* an exposition of the National Board's municipal survey work, described in Chapter VII. All told, an estimated 2,600,000 people were present at 38,000 individual showings of National Board films during 1963. Some 2500 prints are constantly in circulation, and are offered at no charge as a public service.

Another way in which the National Board reaches the public with its fire-safety message is through the home-inspection program carried on by many local fire departments. When a qualified inspector from the fire department goes through a private residence on a fire-prevention inspection tour, he leaves behind an illustrated National

Board folder which reminds the homeowner of the main precautions he should take to prevent fire. Some communities have undertaken a Spring Clean-Up Week, which the National Board has promoted since 1913. In connection with the week, which is observed at various times in different communities, a special folder is published and distributed country-wide. The gist of this spring message is that spring cleaning time is the convenient point in the year at which to dispose of the kind of burnable junk that can start a fire. Beyond that, the clean-up campaign involves replacing faulty house wiring, putting tight lids on flammable paints and oils, and equipping the house with adequate ash trays. The enthusiasm for a clean-up is catching, and an entire household can be not only cleaner but safer after it is done.

The big public campaign of the year is Fire Prevention Week, which takes place in October in the week including October 9, the day of the worst destruction during the great Chicago fire of 1871. It first took form in 1911 as a Fire Prevention Day, when the Association of North American Fire Marshals conceived a commemoration of that anniversary by a special annual effort at public education in fire prevention. The National Board of Fire Underwriters was asked to support the project, which it did with enthusiasm. State governors were all asked to join in the campaign. In 1920 President Wilson issued the first presidential proclamation of Fire Prevention Day, and two years later President Harding proclaimed the first annual Fire Prevention Week in the form that it is now observed. In fact, the proclamation of this event is one of only three presidential proclamations issued regularly each year. Its sponsorship has been broadened to the point where it is now handled by the United States Chamber of Commerce, and the week's activities are carried out in particular by the National Board and by the National Fire Protection Association.

Fire Prevention Week provides an occasion for special efforts, and develops a momentum in public opinion from which the National Board receives extraordinary cooperation in its continuing campaign against fire. In many cities during this week the newspapers, radio, and television stations, school authorities, mayors, fire departments, business associations, and many others join in the war on fire waste. Open house at the local fire station has become an annual fixture at this time of year. Fire Prevention Week has become a minor American tradition, one that is spreading and deepening. Many a parent has for the first time been led by his elementary school-age child into making a fire-safety inspection of the house during Fire Prevention Week, because the youngster caught the enthusiasm for it from his school fire-safety program. In this respect, at least, untold thousands of American homes have seen acted out the old biblical prophecy: "And a little child shall lead them."

Through the years the educational work of the National Board has taken many other forms, such as circulating speakers on fire prevention, providing instructors at university arson seminars, and holding essay contests. One essay contest on the subject of fire prevention that bore notable fruit long after the seed was planted was that held by the National Board in 1921. The contest winner was a Boy Scout living in Oakland, California. Ten years later, a graduate of the United States Military Academy at West Point with a period of army service behind him, he joined the National Board staff as an engineer. In 1950 the same man, Lewis A. Vincent, was chosen as general manager of the National Board of Fire Underwriters to succeed the so-called "Grand Old Man" of the organization, Wilbur A.

Mallalieu. Mr. Vincent remained in the post of general manager until the January 1, 1965, merger which created the new American Insurance Association, of which he became a vice president.

Through its decades of service to the public and to the capital stock fire insurance companies comprising its membership, the National Board has always offered its services to the American government in times of need. In both world wars, particularly, government officials gladly made use of the special knowledge of the National Board in such matters as the protection of Navy yards, Army posts, and supply depots against the dangers of fire and explosion. The engineering skill of the staff members was especially helpful when the country was forced, under great pressure, to produce and ship great quantities of materiel at a time of manpower and equipment shortages. The number of government commendations hanging on the walls of the National Board offices are testimony to the services it rendered to the people through the federal government in those critical times.

Aiding the nation in World Wars I and II meant a virtual transfer of its peacetime activities to a wartime footing. In World War II, for instance, the Engineering Department of the Board assigned practically 100 per cent of its field staff to the protection of those installations where fire or explosion, whether unintentional or sabotage, would have slowed down the prosecution of the war. Special agents of the Arson Department were called upon to assist, and literally hundreds of engineers on the staffs of the insurance inspection bureaus in the forty-eight states participated in this concerted effort. The activity was a voluntary one reimbursed only by a token $1.00 per year paid to the National Board. Staff executives of the Board headed the Advisory Bureaus on Fire Protection established in the offices of the War Department, Department of the Navy, and Coast Guard headquarters.

A testimonial presented by the War Department to the National Board is a fitting expression of appreciation for this phase of the Board's service to the public and to the country. Signed in 1945 by Secretary of War Henry L. Stimson, Army Chief of Staff George C. Marshall, and other high officials, it expresses commendation "for outstanding services rendered to the War Department in the furtherance of the War program." The National Board is praised for having offered its help to the government, "providing a service that could not be secured elsewhere." The officials noted that the resulting fire prevention and protection of military establishments "would have been extremely difficult, if not impossible, without the expert assistance of the National Board of Fire Underwriters."

The United States Navy and the Coast Guard paid tribute in equally generous terms. Behind all the commendations lay a record of technical services, carried out to a large extent by engineers lent to the government by the insurance business. An exact measure of their wartime contribution to the nation can never be made, for it consists of a record of prevention—of fires that never happened.

Because the National Board of Fire Underwriters has been so successful in developing its own program of public services quite independently of government, and has at the same time maintained a close and cordial relationship with government at all levels where mutual interest requires cooperation, the sector of the insurance business that it represents places great importance on preserving its traditional freedom. At the 1964 annual meeting, General Manager Lewis A. Vincent put the issue this way, in discussing the possibility of government intervention into the traditional private areas of the economy:

The insurance business and the federal government have long enjoyed a sympathetic relationship. The facilities of the insurance business have always been available to the authorities and our knowledge and advice in specialized fields have frequently been sought.

Just recently, when a fire and explosion occurred in a processing building at a large atomic energy facility, we were immediately requested by representatives of the Atomic Energy Commission to make available the services of our research director to assist in a study of the occurrence. His findings and recommendations were accepted, and expressions of appreciation have been received for the contribution by this business. We also assisted the National Aeronautical and Space Administration in a review of the safety program developed in connection with the high oxygen environment of space capsules. Our business stands ready, at all times, to extend cooperation for the common good.

We recognize that there are areas which necessarily must be the responsibility of government. But we must insist that those in government recognize that there are limits to those areas and that private enterprise properly conducted must not be unduly restricted by big government... It devolves upon every segment of business and community life to see that any extension of federal power is limited to a sphere that cannot be handled by local government or private business.

Almost from its inception, the National Board of Fire Underwriters was concerned with the regulation of the business of insurance. The executives of the fire insurance companies recognized the business was affected with a common interest long before the courts got around to so deciding.

In the days immediately following the Civil War, when the fire insurance business was moving into a period of major expansion, the state of Virginia undertook to impose a tax on those engaged in this activity. Executives of the member companies of the National Board of Fire Underwriters, believing the business of fire insurance was interstate commerce, challenged the constitutionality of the tax. This case (*Paul v. Virginia*) was carried to the Supreme Court of the United States and the resulting decision became the landmark on which the pattern of regulation for the entire business of insurance was based for approximately 75 years. *Paul v. Virginia* held that insurance was not interstate commerce and therefore the tax in question was constitutional.

Even though this decision was contrary to the views of the National Board of Fire Underwriters, the Board, through its Committee on Laws and its Law Department, assisted in the erection of a pattern of regulation of the business of insurance by the state governments, and that activity continued without interruption until 1944. In that year the Supreme Court of the United States, in the case of *United States v. South-Eastern Underwriters Association,* in effect, reversed *Paul v. Virginia* and held the business of insurance to be commerce and, where it crossed state lines, interstate commerce. If the court had so held in *Paul v. Virginia* some 75 years earlier, when regulation of the business was in its infancy, it would have caused no distress. But coming three-quarters of a century later, after the states had built up systems of regulation based on the court's decisions (approximately a score followed *Paul v. Virginia*)—that insurance was not commerce—the impact of the South-Eastern Underwriters Association decision was nothing short of devastating. Chief Justice Harlan Fiske Stone, in his dissenting opinion in the South-Eastern Underwriters Association case said:

The immediate and only practical effect of the decision now rendered is to withdraw from the states, in large measure, the regulation of insurance and to confer it on the national government, which has adopted no legislative policy and evolved no scheme of regulation with respect to the business of insurance. . . . This court can decide only the questions before it in particular cases. Its action in now overturning the precedents of seventy-five years governing a business of such volume and of such wide ramifications, cannot fail to be the occasion for loosing a flood of litigation and of legislation, state and national, in order to establish a new boundary between state and national power, raising questions which cannot be answered for years to come, during which a great business and the regulatory officers of every state must be harassed by all the doubts and difficulties inseparable from a realignment of the distribution of power in our federal system.

Associate Justice Robert H. Jackson went even further than the Chief Justice, saying:

The Court's decision at very least will require an extensive overhauling of state legislation relating to taxation and supervision. The whole legal basis will have to be reconsidered. What will be irretrievably lost and what may be salvaged no one now can say, and it will take a generation of litigation to determine. Certainly the states lose very important controls and very considerable revenues.

The recklessness of such a course is emphasized when we consider that Congress has not one line of legislation deliberately designed to take over federal responsibility for this important and complicated enterprise. There is no federal department or personnel with national experience in the subject on which Congress can call for counsel in framing regulatory legislation.

In this situation the National Board of Fire Underwriters, through its Committee on Laws, joined with other branches of the business in the formation of an all-industry committee which worked through the National Association of Insurance Commissioners to bring some order out of the chaos.

As a result of this cooperation by all branches of the insurance business, the Congress of the United States passed, and on March 9, 1945, the President of the United States signed, the McCarran-Ferguson Act which became Public Law 15 of the 79th Congress. That Act provided that the continued regulation of the business of insurance by the several states was in the public interest and that silence on the part of Congress should not be construed to impose any barrier to the regulation or taxation of such business by the several states. It further provided that the business of insurance and every person engaged in it should be subject to the laws of the several states which relate to the regulation or taxation of that business. With certain exceptions it suspended the application of the federal antitrust laws until January 1, 1948. In effect this legislation gave the business and the states approximately three years to develop a pattern of nationwide regulation through state legislation, and to the extent such state legislation regulated the business of insurance, federal legislation would not apply.

The problems of reenacting and supplementing regulatory patterns in effect before the South-Eastern Underwriters Association decision were tremendous, but thanks to the cooperative activities of all branches of the business, in which the Committee on Laws of the National Board and the Board's General Counsel, J. Raymond Berry, played a leading part, a nationwide pattern of state legislation was enacted in every state of the union, so expeditiously that the Congress of the United States never felt impelled to enact legislation designed to regulate the business of insurance. At a time when the regulation of nearly every other kind of business seemed to move consistently in the direction of federal control, state regulation of the business of insurance was saved. To accomplish this, conflicting views of those in the business, of those in regulatory positions and those speaking as representatives of the public had to be reconciled in every state before any legislation could be enacted. No one will ever know how many days and nights were spent in this work by the members of the Committee on Laws of the National Board of Fire Underwriters—particularly during the three-year period immediately following the enactment of Public Law 15 of the 79th Congress. The story of the National Board would be less than complete if recognition were not given to the selfless service rendered by these men, not just for their companies, not just for the business of insurance, but basically for the insurance-buying public. Their work is still continuing, as perforce it must. The business of insurance is never static. In the past twenty-five years it has gone through dynamic changes under which the concepts of underwriting by segregated peril have been superseded by the concepts of multiple-line underwriting. These changes in business practices have brought with them the need for changes in regulation by the states and this, in turn, has forced continuous review by the Committee on Laws of the National Board of Fire Underwriters of the regulatory statutes in all the states.

The fact that the pattern of state regulation has continued during this period of revolutionary change in the industry, and while the effectiveness of state regulation was under the constant scrutiny of federal authorities, is a tribute to the quality of the work of the members of the Committee on Laws.

In 1942 the New York State Legislature, seeking the adoption of a standard fire insurance policy, consulted the Law Department and the National Board Committee on Laws for Recommendations and Procedures. The legal men performed such a thorough job that the annual report of the National Board for 1943 characterized their product in this language:

> This new policy is simpler in form, more liberal in its terms, clearer in its expressions, smaller in its size and possesses many advantages over the previous standard policies of New York and over those of most, if not all, of the other States.

Anticipating its adoption in other states, the National Board report continued:

> Its adoption without change by each of the several States would have many advantages and few, if any, disadvantages. Among other things universal adoption would tend toward broader insurance contracts for the benefit of the policyholder; the similarity in wording would be welcomed by those owning property in more than one State; substantial costs of policies and forms would be saved; and, of real importance and desirability, uniformity of the standard policy would tend to greater uniformity of interpretation by the courts, thus tending to reduce litigation.

The prediction by the National Board proved correct to an amazing degree. Within four years almost every state had adopted the New York standard policy form, with only minor variations due to local conditions.

The ninety-eight-and-one-half-year history of the National Board of Fire Underwriters as a separate organization shows it to have remained a pragmatic, practical organization that has felt its way with care and made progress soundly and patiently, step by step. Through most of its lifetime the constitution was changed only in minor particulars, and those changes were made primarily in order to meet new needs and new situations. So it was that in the early 1960s it became clear to many insurance executives active in National Board affairs that several of its functions were being duplicated by the Association of Casualty and Surety Companies. Many of the companies belonged to both organizations, since the day had long passed when fire insurance companies were restricted to writing that kind of policy alone. In fact, insurance men frequently made trips to New York to attend double meetings of committees of two organizations that might just as well have been combined. For several years, therefore, a spirit of unity was in the air when fire insurance men gathered at 85 John Street in New York, and when casualty men gathered in the adjoining building at 110 William Street. Steadily the two groups drew closer until the merger was finally agreed upon in 1964.

Addressing the last annual meeting of the National Board in May of that year, President Clarke Smith outlined numerous steps by which the fire insurance business had adjusted itself to new developments, and had sought unity with others where conditions justified such a step. One example was the concentration of diverse public-relations activities in the Insurance Information Institute. Another was the creation of the Insurance Data Processing Center, where electronic data-processing facilities would provide broadened service to the industry and the millions of policyholders.

Addressing himself directly to the forthcoming merger of 1965, President Smith continued:

Just as the common interests of fire insurance companies led to the establishment of the National Board of Fire Underwriters in 1866, so do the common interests of the property and casualty business today point toward a closer relationship. The Board's Executive Committee, in April 1962, recorded itself as favoring a combination of the major associations. Since then there have been many meetings of the committee appointed to study the problems attendant upon such a merger.

At the annual meeting of the Association of Casualty and Surety Companies, President Ridgway told of the proposed combination of the National Board of Fire Underwriters and the Association of Casualty and Surety Companies, thereby creating an entirely new over-all trade organization. Changes in the nature of the business to multiple-line powers make this move feasible and necessary, and such a new trade organization will be an important force for service to its members and the public.

In a consolidated organization, we can look forward to a combination of functions where feasible, a realignment of functions where practicable, streamlining of operations, and a reduction of expense by over-all economies. The result will be an organization strong in support of the membership from which it draws its own strength.

At its final annual meeting the National Board reported 186 member companies, a group representing a far greater influence and combination of resources than the small number that gathered in 1866 to form a permanent, national organization of fire insurance companies. By odd coincidence, the National Board's independent history started and ended with two Smiths: President Clarke Smith of the Royal-Globe Insurance Companies held the gavel at the end, nearly a century after President J. Milton Smith of the Arctic Fire Insurance Company had moved the appointment of the original committee on organization.

The transformation of the National Board of Fire Underwriters into a constituent part of the American Insurance Association necessarily implied numerous changes in officers, in committees, in staff, in staff duties. The Actuarial Bureau of the National Board was scheduled to become independent of the AIA, under the title National Insurance Actuarial and Statistical Association, and to expand the scope of its activities. Special agents of the Arson, Theft and Fraud Department were to be trained to handle casualty work and the special agents of the Claims Bureau of the former Association of Casualty and Surety Companies were to be trained in the type of investigation handled by the NBFU men. Step by step the activities of the two organizations were to be integrated into one smoothly working program.

The physical merging of the staffs symbolized the final unity of the new American Insurance Association. Henceforth the AIA would confront the problems that lay ahead on behalf of a stronger, more united insurance business. Already it faced challenges of tremendous scope and complexity, for which it had been prepared over long years of increasingly responsible service since the birth of the National Board of Fire Underwriters. In 1866 it came to life when a firecracker set off a conflagration that devastated Portland, Maine. In 1966 it faces the problem of enabling a much greater population to live safely with atomic power, with jet-powered aircraft, with hundreds of new chemicals, with high values concentrated in huge warehouses, and with dense urbanization.

Yet while its separate existence has come to an end, the National Board of Fire Underwriters lives on in the hearts and memories of those who knew it best. The following passage taken from an editorial in *Fire Engineering*, written in tribute and final salute to the National Board, might stand as a fitting elegy:

> The "National Board," as it is referred to by the fire service, has been considered the oldest business association in the nation. Formed in 1866, it has come to be recognized as the one organization outside the fire service in which fire officers have for years placed the utmost confidence....
>
> To all those acquainted with the work of this organization it will continue to be known in fire-service terminology as the "National Board" for at least another generation. A spontaneous tribute of respect of this nature has to be earned. In this case it is the result of nearly a century of genuine service.

INDEX

About the Author

A. L. Todd is a writer of nonfiction books and articles who specializes in history, biography and public affairs. He is particularly interested in the contributions of unusual men and organizations to the rational development of human society. A native of Washington, D. C., Mr. Todd carried out his research for several years in the Library of Congress before moving to New York City, his present home. A graduate of the Phillips Exeter Academy and Swarthmore College, he was a teacher and news reporter before turning to fulltime writing. Mr. Todd and his wife, Jean G. Todd, a physiologist, have two grown sons, Paul and Philip.